TWAYNE'S WORLD AUTHORS SERIES

A Survey of the World's Literature

Sylvia E. Bowman, Indiana University

GENERAL EDITOR

RUSSIA

Nicholas P. Vaslef, U.S. Air Force Academy

EDITOR

Alexander Bestuzhev-Marlinsky

TWAS 344

Александр Петрофисъ

Alexander
Bestuzhev-Marlinsky

By LAUREN G. LEIGHTON
Northern Illinois University, DeKalb

TWAYNE PUBLISHERS
A DIVISION OF G. K. HALL & CO., BOSTON

Library of Congress Cataloging in Publication Data

Leighton, Lauren G.
    Alexander Bestuzhev-Marlinsky.

    (Twayne's world authors series, TWAS 344. Russia)
    Bibliography: p. 150.
    1.   Bestuzhev, Aleksandr Aleksandrovich, 1797-1837.
PG3321.B45Z73   891.7'8'309   74-19225
IBSN 0-8057-2149-5

MANUFACTURED IN THE UNITED STATES OF AMERICA

Contents

About the Author

Lauren G. Leighton is an Associate Professor of Russian and Acting Chairman of the Department of Foreign Languages and Literatures of Northern Illinois University. He received his M. A. in Slavic Languages and Literatures and Russian Area Certificate at Indiana University in 1962, and his Ph. D. in Slavic Languages at the University of Wisconsin in 1968. A specialist primarily in Russian Romanticism, he has published articles, reviews, and translations in *Canadian Slavic Studies*, *The Horn Book Magazine*, *New Literary History*, *Russian Literature*, *Russian Literature Triquarterly*, *Science and Public Affairs*, *The Slavic and East European Journal*, *The Slavonic Review*, and *Soviet Studies in Literature*. His fiction and translations of modern Russian fiction have appeared in *The Chicago Review*, *Descant*, *The Malahat Review*, *Prairie Schooner*, *Russian Literature Triquarterly*, and *Spirit* under the name Larry Gregg. A study of Romantic criticism, history, and theory, *Russian Romanticism: Two Essays*, is forthcoming from Mouton Publishers (The Hague). He is currently working on a translation with commentaries of Russian Romantic essays and a study of numerology in Russian literature.

Preface

The Romantic period is perhaps the most crucial stage in the history of Russian literature. It is the time when the most essential problems of the development of a national literature — the questions of form and style, criticism and theory, method and technique — were approached for the first time by an effectively large number of talented and dedicated men of letters. During this period, Russians took the fullest advantage of the cultural achievements of the eighteenth century to lay the groundwork for the great literature that flourished in the later Realist period. The Russians now ceased to merely imitate European values and began to systematically adapt them to their own national experience. Russian literature did not gain an international standing during the Romantic period, but it was blessed with the talents of some of the most creative men in the history of Russian letters, and three of these men — Pushkin, Gogol, and Lermontov — later came to be counted among the world's best writers and poets.

Alexander Bestuzhev, pseudonym Marlinsky, occupies an important place among the men who shaped the Romantic movement during its peak years, the 1820's and 1830's. It would be difficult to find a literary figure more representative of Russian Romanticism than Alexander Bestuzhev-Marlinsky. He was the most eager of all his contemporaries to lay claim to the title Romantic, to search out and assimilate the values he considered Romantic, to cultivate the trends usually associated with Romanticism, to commit himself totally, without reservations, to the most extravagant qualities of the Romantic manner. His life, his ideas, his opinions, his poetry, his prose tales, his style — all are Romantic, even ultra-Romantic. He is Russia's Romantic extremist, an exaggerated and therefore a remarkably clear-cut manifestation of the nature of Russian Romanticism. The name Marlinsky and the term Marlinism have become synonyms for Romanticism in Russia, and this synonymity has impressed Russians from Belinsky to Turgenev and Tolstoy, to the Modernists who went back to Romanticism for their roots, to present-day Soviet scholars.

Neither the nature of Russian Romanticism, nor the Romantic movement as a whole is the prime purpose of this book, but a study of Bestuzhev-Marlinsky can offer a great deal both to Slavicists concerned with Russian Romanticism and to non-Slavicists who have a comparative literary interest in the period. This is all the more true because it was not Pushkin, Gogol, or Lermontov who were the most popular and typical writers of their time, but Bestuzhev-Marlinsky. If, as has been asserted, the nature of a national literature is to be discovered at its secondary level rather than at its peaks, then this Russian Romantic is an ideal choice for an American book, and it is time for him to become better known outside his own country.

As for his own country, there can be no doubt that Bestuzhev-Marlinsky has remained a viable subject of interest. He is acknowledged as the first Russian writer to enjoy a more than minor vogue in Europe, and his works were even published in complete collections in the major European languages in the 1840's and 1850's. His prose tales were plagiarized by Alexandre Dumas, père, and his best known tale, *Ammalat-bek*, was the second Russian literary work published in the United States. At home he was an exciting experience in the adolescence of great Russian writers: Tolstoy and Turgenev recalled his prose tales with unabashed nostalgia, and Alexey Remizov used to declaim the prose tales purely for their sound effects. Advertisements for inexpensive editions of his tales were a feature of Russian newspapers until well after 1917 — an indication that he remained popular with the less sophisticated Russian reader. In this sense he was Russia's Scott, Dumas, or Cooper: that particular writer who became his country's most favorite writer without becoming seriously recognized.

Editions of Bestuzhev-Marlinsky's collected works have been published regularly every two or three decades; appropriate anthologies of prose, poetry, criticism, or sociopolitical essays are not considered complete without the inclusion of one or two of his works; editions of his works in 1937 and 1958 enjoyed large sales in the Soviet Union; his writings have been the subject of some of the most prominent Russian scholars of the past century and a half, and Soviet scholars continue to take a keen interest in his heritage and his place in the history of Russian literature.

Above all, Bestuzhev-Marlinsky merits a book on his own grounds. It would be difficult to find another Russian who led a more fascinating life: controversial critic and fierce polemicist; imaginative writer of prose tales; passing fair poet; translator; reliable historian, political commentator, ethnographer, natural scientist, and linguist; political conspirator and revolutionary idealist, as well as leader of the Decembrist revolt of 1825; martyred exile to Siberia and the Caucasus; daredevil soldier and friend of mountain bandits; and suspected murderer of his alleged child mistress — all this capped by a violent death in battle which has remained a mystery to this day. His prose tales — the source of his great popularity — can be appreciated for their adventure-packed plots, implausible situations, melodramatic narration, brave heroes, charming heroines, variegated themes, ultra-Romantic style. He was an excellent craftsman, without ever becoming a great writer, and his works do not lack for materials requiring serious critical attention. His activities as a critic of the 1820's reveal a great deal about the literature of the time, and his poetry tells much about Russian Romantic creativity. Finally, Bestuzhev was a knowledgeable theorist of Romantic esthetics. He is thus a fascinating, as well as a necessary, subject for a book.

LAUREN G. LEIGHTON

Northern Illinois University, DeKalb

Acknowledgments

I would like to express my gratitude to those who helped me to complete this work. Research in Madison, Wisconsin, New York City, Helsinki, Leningrad, Marburg an der Lahn, and Munich was made possible by a University of Wisconsin Research Grant, 1965 - 66, summer 1967, an NDEA-related Fulbright-Hays award, 1966 - 67, and participation in the US-USSR academic exchange under the auspices of the International Research and Exchanges Board and the Ministry of Secondary and Higher Education of the USSR, spring 1970. Much good advice was given by two good friends, Pierre R. Hart and H. William Chalsma. I am equally grateful for advice to many scholars in Leningrad and Moscow, particularly those who have devoted so much care to the heritage of Alexander Bestuzhev-Marlinsky. To my wife, Hera, I am indebted for countless hours of proofreading, corrections, editing, criticism, and advice, and for her patience and impatience. This book began with two papers written in seminars conducted by Professors Xenia Gasiorowski and J. Thomas Shaw of the University of Wisconsin, and with my doctoral dissertation written under the latter's guidance. Without Professor Shaw's generous advice, to say nothing of the many hours he spent on the several drafts of dissertation and book, this work would not have been published. It is with appreciation and respect, therefore, that I dedicate this book to him.

Chronology

1797   October 23, Alexander Alexandrovich Bestuzhev born in St. Petersburg.

1806   Enrolled in Cadet Corps of Engineers.

1817   Joins Light Dragoon Regiment. Publishes first translations and lyric poems.

1819   Publishes two devastating reviews of plays by Prince A. A. Shakhovskoy and P. A. Katenin.

1820   Uses pseudonym Marlinsky for first time in an anonymous review. Becomes member of prestigious *Free Society of Lovers of Russian Letters*.

1821   *Journey to Revel* published as book. First prose tales — *Gedeon* and *Castle Wenden* — published.

1822   Appointed adjutant to court adviser General Augustine A. Betancourt. Becomes regular contributor to leading journals.

1823   *Roman and Olga* published. Begins publishing literary almanac *The Polar Star* with Kondraty Ryleev. Recruited by Ryleev into Northern Society.

1824   *Castle Neihausen* published. Becomes member of Northern Society's ruling *duma*.

1825   *Tournament at Revel* and *The Traitor* published. Plans several attempts on life of Alexander I. Helps plan armed uprising following death of Alexander I in late November. Incites Moscow Regiment to revolt on December 14 and holds it in position on Senate Square. Surrenders to commandant of Winter Palace on December 15.

1826   Ryleev and four other Decembrist leaders hanged on July 13. Bestuzhev sent to Fort Slava in Finland in August.

1827   Reaches Yakutsk on Christmas Eve to begin Siberian exile.

1828   Studies foreign languages. Writes best lyric poetry. Meets Georg Adolph Erman, a German scientist who educates him in the natural sciences.

1829   Transferred to Caucasus as a common soldier.

1830   Essay "Letter to Doctor Erman" and prose tale *The Test* published. Becomes regular contributor to journals of Literary Plebeians.

1831   *Lieutenant Belozor* and *The Terrible Divination* published. Brother Pyotr wounded in battle and driven insane.

1832   *The Frigate "Hope"*, *The Raiders*, *The Red Cape*, *The Cuirassier*, and *Ammalat-bek* published. Olga Nestertsova killed in his bed.

1833   Essay "On N. Polevoy's Novel *The Oath on the Tomb of the Lord*" published. First complete collected works published.

1834   Begins novel *Vadimov*. V. G. Belinsky begins anti-Marlinsky campaign.

1836   *Mulla Nur* published. Transferred to "death post" on Caspian Sea.

1837   Systematic persecution, continual illness, and news of Pushkin's death in a duel provoke thoughts and writings of death in battle. June 7: Killed in skirmish with mountaineers at Cape Adler on the Caspian Sea.

CHAPTER 1

Alexander Bestuzhev-Marlinsky

"NOWADAYS all are on their knees before him," complained the critic Belinsky in 1834, "[and] if they are not all in one voice calling him a *Russian Balzac*, it is only because they fear to demean him thereby, and expect the French to call Balzac a *French Marlinsky*."[1] Although he has long since been eclipsed by his more famous contemporary Pushkin, Alexander Bestuzhev-Marlinsky enjoyed an unprecedented popularity with the Russian reading public of the 1830's and reigned as an almost undisputed favorite. "We all loved Marlinsky frightfully," recalled one of his readers, "for his dashing and courtly heroes, for what seemed to us a magnificent ardor of feeling, and finally for his brilliant and whirling language. . . . We doted on Marlinsky with boundless delight."[2] "It was not on Pushkin that the public attention of that time was concentrated," asserted Turgenev later in the nineteenth century, "Marlinsky still basked in the reputation of most beloved writer."[3]

I *His Early Life: St. Petersburg*

If any Russian of the early nineteenth century was suited by personality, by talent, and by literary manner to become the most beloved writer of Russia's first significantly large reading public, it was Alexander Alexandrovich Bestuzhev. He was born in 1797, the fifth child of the five sons and three daughters of Alexander F. Bestuzhev, military officer, writer, pedagogue, and leader of the Russian Enlightenment.[4] Although Alexander F. Bestuzhev had married the daughter of a merchant, and the Bestuzhev children never escaped this stigma, the Bestuzhev family was of ancient lineage and otherwise of good social standing in St. Petersburg circles. The children were educated at home under their father's supervision and were noted for their social brilliance. They had free access to their father's extensive library, became voracious readers, and three of the sons became writers. Their family life seems to have been one of incessant intellectual stimulation, and they were raised to excel at literary efforts. When only nine years old, Alexander wrote a five-act play for puppets with the romantic title *The Enchanted Forest*, and even his older brothers acknowledged him to be the family leader of imaginative games and collective literary projects. According to the testimonies of his brothers and sisters, he was also an impulsive and emotional child, and no one was surprised when he later took part in the ill-starred revolt of December 14, 1825. Nor did any member of his family ever detect any discrepancy between his temperamental personality and the unrestrained style of his prose tales.

All five of the Bestuzhev brothers became military officers, and four of them became political revolutionaries. Alexander's military education began in 1806, and although he dreamed of following his older brother Nikolay into an adventurous naval career, and even spent several summers at sea, in 1817 he was admitted into the elite Light Dragoon Regiment in St. Petersburg. His enthusiasm and wit quickly won attention, and he was marked by his superiors as a popular leader of soldiers and promising staff officer. In 1820 and 1821 he accompanied his regiment to Poland and Revel (now Tallin, capital of Estonia) — journeys well documented in his first prose tales and historical travel accounts. In 1822 he was appointed adjutant to Augustine A. Betancourt, one of Tsar Alexander's influential military advisors, and in the next three years, even though there was no war in which to win swift military glory, it seemed there could be no limits to the fine career awaiting him in the army and at court. His connections in the whirl of St. Petersburg society were impeccable, and his Circassian-like features — black curly hair, flashing black eyes, slender figure — made him a favorite at court balls and in the homes of eligible young women.

Nor was his military career his only promise of brilliance. In 1817 his first poetry, translations, and historical essays began to appear in leading journals and he established a reputation as a translator of works from French, German, and English. Then, in 1819, he published two articles attacking the leading figures of the Russian theater, the dramatists Prince Alexander A. Shakhovskoy and Pavel A. Katenin. The flamboyance of his style and the vicious wit of his criticisms made him an immediate sensation. During the next six years, in literary criticism and translations, in poetry, and in his first prose tales, Bestuzhev climbed to the top of literary circles.

Throughout this period his polemical articles appeared in leading journals under the signatures "A. Bestuzhev," "A. B.," or, in one instance, "A. Marlinsky," a name he took from the Marli pavilion at Peterhof.[5] Together with such men as Orest Somov, Prince Pyotr A. Vyazemsky, Nikolay Grech, Faddey Bulgarin, Kondraty Ryleev, Evgeny A. Baratynsky, and Alexander S. Pushkin, he became a proponent of that diverse intellectual grouping known as "the new, the modern, the so-called Romantic school." From 1823 to 1825, he published the annual literary almanac *Polyarnaya zvezda* ("The Polar Star"), with the poet Kondraty Ryleev, making it a triumphant voice of Romantic thought in Russia. Through his series of "Glances" at Russian literature, which stated the almanac's editorial position, he influenced public literary taste for three important years and set a standard of opinion which had consequences lasting many years beyond.[6] Until the appearance in 1825 of Baron Anton A. Delvig's *Severnye Tsvety* ("Northern Flowers"), the literary almanac of the Pushkin Pleiad, *The Polar Star* attracted some of the most important literary works of the best writers of the time. During these six years, which represent the first of two periods·in Bestuzhev's career, with his Siberian exile intervening, he divided his time between court and military duties and literary meetings in St. Petersburg apartments. It was a swift life, and Bestuzhev lived it impetuously, racing through St. Petersburg from event to event to event.

The variety of his acquaintances during these years is amazing, and they testify to his prominence in the 1820's. His reputation in the army and at court reached even Tsar Alexander I and his brothers, the Grand Dukes Constantine and Nicholas. In literary circles he was accepted by the older generation, the Karamzinians of the so-called Sentimental-Elegiac School — Vasily A. Zhukovsky, Konstantin N. Batyushkov, Nikolay I. Gnedich, Vasily L. Pushkin, and of course Nikolay M. Karamzin himself, the writer of Sentimental prose tales and official national historian. In 1818 he met the publishers Nikolay I. Grech and Faddey V. Bulgarin, with whom he maintained close ties even after they later became leaders of the reactionary press and, reputedly, agents for the secret police of Nicholas I. In 1821 or 1822 he fell under the influence of the political idealist and poet Kondraty F. Ryleev, and in 1822 he began a correspondence with Prince Pyotr A. Vyazemsky, already a recognized champion of Romanticism. In the winter of 1823-24 he carried on a literary feud with both the Shishkovites, the followers of the linguistic archaist Admiral Alexander S. Shishkov, and the Katenin circle, the more conservative Romantics led by Pavel A. Katenin and including, among others, the poet Wilhelm K. Küchelbecker and the playwright Alexander S. Griboedov. Bestuzhev first disliked Griboedov for his identification with Katenin, but in 1825 the two men met and became close friends. In 1823 Bestuzhev met Evgeny A. Baratynsky, perhaps the second greatest poet of the day after Pushkin, and in 1825 he and Ryleev edited Baratynsky's first collected poems. In 1824 he met Nikolay A. Polevoy, soon to become publisher of the journal *Moscow Telegraph* and author of the four-volume *History of the Russian People* (1829-33). His friendship with Polevoy was perhaps as close as his friendship with Ryleev; in Polevoy's journal, under the editorship of the younger brother Ksenofont A. Polevoy, he published his best tales of the 1830's. His path never crossed Pushkin's, but in the year 1825 he and Ryleev carried on a correspondence with Pushkin, resulting in several published and unpublished essays by all three men on some of the most vital problems posed by the development of Romanticism in Russia. The two editors published parts of the first chapter of *Eugene Onegin* in their almanac and at the time of their arrest were negotiating to purchase the rights to the remainder of the famous novel in verse. Bestuzhev's involvement in the Decembrist conspiracy brought him into close association with other Decembrists — a roll-call of some of the most brilliant political thinkers, literary figures, and army officers of the time.

The greatest problem in understanding Bestuzhev's character is that the dramatic events of his life and the legend of Marlinsky overwhelm reality. He rushed through the early 1820's in a whirl of social activities at court, the fuss and fury of the literary war over Romanticism, and the duties of an ambitious young dragoon officer. His role and participation in the Decembrist conspiracy and revolt gained him a notoriety which has lasted to this day. His imprisonment and exile to Siberia tinged his reputation with an aura of convict, political martyr, and brooding exile. The appearance of his first mature prose tales in the early 1830's raised him to heights of popularity beyond even those attained by Pushkin in the 1820's. During the 1830's, in the Caucasus as a common soldier, he became a pure *Kavkazets*, a Russian who spoke and lived like a native among the Caucasian peoples. During the same years he distinguished himself for bravery in battles with the mountaineers, and his reputation among hero-worshipping young officers was enhanced all the more by the humiliations inflicted on him by a spiteful government. In 1833 he gained further notoriety as a Don Juan when an adolescent girl, rumored to be his mistress, died violently in his bed. His ability to vanish into the mountains and to pass as a Caucasian makes one wonder what his relations with the bandits and rebels really were: were his sympathies once again in opposition to his loyalty to his government, or was he a spy? And finally, his tragic and mysterious death in battle — was it suicide or murder by official decree? — gave rise to a legend which has fascinated Russians ever since.

The facets of his personality which come most clearly to the fore are his impetuousity and passion. N. A. Kotlyarevsky, who wrote Bestuzhev's biography, defined this part of his character when he noted:

Alexander Alexandrovich was a literary man of very lively and impetuous temperament. At any given moment of his life, when some thought popped into his head, or some feeling overwhelmed him, he swiftly seized his pen and wrote hastily, as if fearing to lose the freshness of the impression. Marlinsky was unable to think about something for long, to develop and dissect a thought in detail, to smooth and polish a phrase in which a thought should have been embodied, to nurture a feeling for long or dress it in outward finery more or less in keeping with its force and essence. He was all impetuosity and urgency, and everything he wrote was the uncompromised, swift echo of his very life or of the poetic notion he had of it. . . . Throughout [his works] there can be felt a man who is in haste. . . .[7]

His impetuosity can be felt with particular force in his keen love of politics, a love to which he devoted much of his life, both before and after the Decembrist revolt. In a letter of 1824 to P. A. Vyazemsky he wrote: "I must confess to you, Prince, that I have devoted myself keenly to politics; yes, and how can one not love it in our time — this science of rights, men, and peoples, this magnificent, immutable standard of *thine* and *mine,* this sacred torch of truth in the gloom of ignorance and the dungeon of autocracy."[8] Closely united with his political interests was his concern for nation, history, ethnography, and languages — all that goes under the heading of the Russian concept of *narodnost'* and which, as must be shown, figured prominently in his literary contributions. Although he was far too impatient to be a true scholar, he had a voracious appetite for a wide variety of subjects and plunged himself with no discipline or method into whatever subject interested him at the moment. He had a gift for mastering the customs, history, and languages of whatever people he found himself among, and he gained a lasting reputation as an authority on the Baltic area, then Siberia, and finally the Caucasus. He wrote essays and travel accounts about all three of these areas of the Empire, and his authority was buttressed by his ability to master languages quickly. Within a year of his arrival in the Caucasus he had mastered both Persian and Tatar (the Turkic dialects), and this helped him to disappear into the mountains and live as a native Tatar, Circassian, or Kabardinian. One of his memoirist-admirers, Ya. I. Kostenetsky, has testified to this point:

> Bestuzhev knew Persian and Tatar very well and spoke them with perfect fluency. He was acquainted with almost the whole population of Derbent and because of his generous nature never refused aid by word or deed to any needy Asiatic. . . . All the residents of Derbent loved and esteemed him, and when he left Derbent almost the whole city populace accompanied him on horse and foot more than twenty versts from the city, firing their guns and lighting torches along the way. Musicians beat their drums and played their instruments, others sang and danced, and in general the whole crowd tried in every way to express its regard for its beloved "Iskender-Bey."[9]

Bestuzhev actually taught his native friends to read and write their own language, and he was admired locally for his knowledge of Persian literature.

His ability to learn a foreign language has been praised over and over again, and languages play a central role in his style and diction. From the beginning of his literary career Bestuzhev was able to speak French and English, he quickly gained fluency in Polish, and he read extensively in German. Among the other languages he used in his early works are Ancient Greek, Latin, Spanish, Dutch, Lithuanian, and Estonian. During his Siberian exile he further perfected his knowledge of English, French, and German, and he taught himself Italian in order to read Dante in the original. He learned to speak Yakut, and his knowledge of this Turkic dialect enabled him to plunge into the study of the Caucasian dialects even before leaving Siberia. Part of his early career was devoted to translation of critical and historical works from English, French, and German, and he translated poetry from the latter two languages, as well as from Azeri, Georgian, Circassian, and Persian. While in Siberia he translated a ballad from Yakut.

II The Revolt of December 14, 1825

December 14, 1825 — the day of the insurrection that later came to be known as the Decembrist revolt — was undoubtedly the most important in Bestuzhev's life. Two years earlier he had been recruited by Ryleev into the Northern Society of the Decembrist movement, where he quickly became a leader of the Society's radical left wing.[10] Thus, all the time that he had been leading a full public life and cultivating two careers, he had also been busy with political conspiracy, with the first modern attempt to overthrow the autocracy and end the rule of the Romanov dynasty. On the day of the revolt Bestuzhev led the Moscow Regiment onto Senate Square in St. Petersburg in a hastily contrived plan to prevent Nicholas I from ascending the throne. He was one of the most decisive rebel leaders of the day and the only officer who kept his troops orderly and militarily effective. He waited throughout that cold winter day, and only when the government's cannons scattered the rebels did he abandon the Square. He understood immediately that the revolt had failed and believed that failure had proved that his act of idealism was treason. He returned home, burned his papers, donned his full-dress uniform, and surrendered to the commandant of the Winter Palace — his own duty post. He seems to have made up his mind about his post-revolt behavior in advance, for during the ensuing official investigation he cooperated frankly and fully with the authorities. The laconic findings of the investigation commission sum up the bare facts of his role in the conspiracy: "Staff Captain of the Light Dragoon Regiment A. Bestuzhev, age 27. By his own admission he deliberated regicide and the extermination of the Imperial Family; he incited others to that end; he also agreed to deprive the Imperial Family of its freedom; he took part in the planning of the revolt by persuading his comrades and by composing incendiary verses and songs. He personally took part in the rebellion and incited the lower ranks to that end."[11] Bestuzhev spent the remainder of his life in incarceration, Siberian exile, and service as a common soldier in the Caucasus.

Russians of the later nineteenth century were intensely curious about the Decembrist revolt and the behavior of the rebels following its failure. The Decembrists became sacred martyrs and revolutionary heroes, but it was not until the 1920's that the Soviet government brought much of the truth to light by publishing the records of the official investigation.[12] These records reveal a mixed reaction: while some of the Decembrists remained uncooperative and defiant at great personal cost, others eagerly betrayed their comrades, either from opportunism or from cowardice. Two of Bestuzhev's brothers, Nikolay and Mikhail, were exiled unrepentant to Siberia, and Kondraty Ryleev died on the gallows with four others of the chief leadership. Others received less harsh punishment for their cooperation. Many of the Decembrists were made to confess after months of cruel mental distress, and by treatment calculated to exploit their demoralization; some cooperated with realistic fatalism, yet with honor and concern for their comrades; many lied to protect themselves and others. Bestuzhev's behavior is once again a choice between extreme possibilities.

Soviet historians have tended to interpret Bestuzhev as a committed revolutionary and an uncooperative prisoner,[13] but the record reveals a situation far more complex than this. The fact is that he had become dubious about the methods of the conspirators, and although he was committed to the Decembrist ideals and acted decisively during the revolt, he seems undeniably to have made up his mind to atone for his actions as best he could. A confidential letter written to Nicholas I following his arrest is considered to be one of the most lucid and frank statements by a Decembrist about the social, historical, and political causes of the movement.[14] He managed to withhold certain facts, particularly those related to his brothers, but he provided evidence about both the details and the general nature of the conspiracy. His testimony was thorough and his evidence may well have sent his friend Ryleev to the gallows. To avoid this possibility is to deny the tragedy of his predicament and obscure the meaning of a desperate effort to act honorably in a situation that left no room for honor.

In the 1860's the historian Mikhail I. Semevsky won the confidence of the Bestuzhev family, and in the next two decades he published the letters, articles, and memoirs that have since been organized into the Bestuzhev family archives.[15] In discussing a letter of Bestuzhev in which he joked about his inability to say no, Semevsky noted: "It is very possible that in this jest A. Bestuzhev alludes to his loquacity during the investigation of the affair of December 14. While his brothers Nikolay and Mikhail, firmly convinced that they could expect the death penalty, considered it superfluous to succumb under interrogation to garrulity, and usually limited their answers to 'I do not know,' 'No,' and so on, Alexander, because of his lively and ardent temperament, went into detailed explanations of the aims of the secret society and his part in it. His frankness was the reason his lot was eased: instead of penal servitude he was exiled to a settlement. . . . "[16]

The rewards for confession were great — not the least of these was the later opportunity to return to an active literary life in 1830 — but to assume that Bestuzhev belongs among those Decembrists who betrayed for gain or for fear is again a misleading simplification. What may and must be said about his testimony is that while he did not volunteer information, he did not avoid providing it when pushed. He strove to protect his brothers, even attempting to take their blame on himself, and he tried to give the impression of them and himself as reluctant, even inactive revolutionaries.[17] He emphasized those parts of his role which could not but be appreciated by the government. He convinced the investigators that, whatever the reasons which prompted him to join the Northern Society — his hatred of serfdom, his dissatisfaction with the increasingly stifling and inefficient regime of Alexander I, his dreams of a more humane society and state, and his conviction that the national aspirations of the Russian people were not being realized under the autocracy — he soon became disillusioned by the shallow and impractical behavior of some of his fellow conspirators. He insisted that he had wanted to leave the Society long before December 14, but was drawn deeper into the conspiracy against his own better judgment.[18]

When asked, "What reasons induced you to join the secret society?" Bestuzhev replied: "In joining the society, out of youthful delusion and my impetuous imagination, I thought thereby to be of use to my fatherland at a future date. . . . The lure of novelty and mystery played an equal part in this, and little by little seduced me into criminal ideas."[19] Elaborating on this point, he stated: "From the age of nineteen I had begun reading liberal books, and this turned my head. For that matter, not possessing any positive conceptions of my own, I shouted into the wind, like all young men, without any purpose whatever. In 1822 . . . I made friends with Ryleev . . . and we dreamed together, and with his fervid imagination he seduced me even further."[20]

In placing blame on Ryleev, Bestuzhev was stating a fact he could not avoid. He and Ryleev were known to be close friends, and Ryleev had committed himself so totally to the conspiracy and revolt that there could be no escape for him. Kondraty Ryleev was a powerful personality — his poetry, letters, and testimony reveal him as a fanatical idealist — and Bestuzhev had been under his influence for over three years. They had collaborated on many literary projects, including *The Polar Star*. Bestuzhev occupied a bachelor apartment in the home of Ryleev and his wife, and they had long since formed a secret alliance within the Northern Society. "Although he was my very best friend," Bestuzhev confessed, "for the sake of the truth I will not hide the fact that he was the chief instigator of the adventure [i.e., the revolt itself]; by enflaming everyone with his poetic imagination and fortifying them with his persistence."[21] Ryleev, asserted Bestuzhev, recruited him into the Northern Society in 1824 (it has since been proved that the recruitment took place a full year earlier).[22] Because of Ryleev's influence and his constant reproaches, he had joined the Society's ruling *duma;* it was Ryleev who insisted that he attend meetings he would otherwise have avoided; and it was Ryleev's persistence that made him an active recruiter of new members into the Society.[23]

Ryleev also drew him into the most extreme activities of the Northern Society. The Northerners, generally less radical than the members of the Southern Society, vaguely agreed on the introduction of a constitutional monarchy and were on record as opposing the Southerners' plans for a republic. St. Petersburg was closer to the autocracy than the headquarters of the Southern Society (near Kiev), and the Northerners were apprehensive of such Southern plans as assassination. Ryleev, on the other hand, was more in agreement with the plans of the Southern Society, and he worked covertly, with Bestuzhev's help, to subordinate the Northern Society to the Southern aims. Thus, Bestuzhev confessed, he aided Ryleev in attempts to subvert the Northern Society and consistently supported Ryleev's conviction that a revolution must be planned. It was through his offices that Ryleev succeeded in recruiting the services of two assassins, Yakubovich and Kakhovskoy, and he also agreed to Ryleev's plans to assassinate Alexander I and exterminate the Imperial family. In true conspiratorial style, these aims were kept secret from the majority of the members of the Northern Society: they represented a conspiracy within a conspiracy, a plan within a plan, and they were known only to the members of an inner circle. When Alexander I suddenly died, Bestuzhev helped Ryleev persuade the reluctant Northerners to take advantage of confusion over the legitimate heir to the throne and carry out the hastily contrived revolt. And it was Bestuzhev who played the decisive role on Senate Square by inciting the key Moscow Regiment and holding it in position all through the tense confrontation with the Tsar.[24] All of this, Bestuzhev insisted, he had done without conviction that his cause was just: "When I went after the Moscow Regiment I first prayed to God with hot tears — 'If our cause is just, help us . . . if not, let Thy will be done.' I now know His will — but the hand of God and the wrath of my Tsar bear heavily upon me. . . . I feel now that I have abused my talents, but that by my saber or pen I could still bring honor to my fatherland — to live usefully and die honorably for my Sovereign!"[25]

The statement is melodramatic and self-serving, but it is also true. Having failed in an affair whose ideals he doubted in part and whose practical military realization he doubted in entirety, Bestuzhev had clearly resolved in advance to carry out his duty to his comrades, and, in the event of failure, to atone as best he could, as bravely as he could, as honorably as such a nebulous situation permitted. While remaining silent about the actions of almost all but Ryleev, and while deriving strength from the undeniable fact that he had remained steadfast to the end of the revolt, he decided to make a clean breast of his actions. He did not volunteer information that would incriminate anyone but Ryleev, he did not attempt to spare himself at anyone's expense, and his testimony was substantiated by others. His testimony about Ryleev's actions was true; it could scarcely have been avoided, and he was able to prove that he had serious reservations about some of Ryleev's most extreme plans. The most salient example of this latter fact is to be found in his testimony that he disapproved of regicide and worked behind Ryleev's back to dissuade both Yakubovich and Kakhovskoy from assassinating Nicholas I. He repeated this testimony on several occasions, even in a confrontation with Ryleev, and both assassins substantiated his assertions.[26] Of all the personal devils borne by the Decembrists in the ordeal of the investigation, his was among the most cruel: he betrayed his closest friend. But if this is so, it is also true that his dilemma was unavoidable. The fact that he had remained true to the conspiracy to the bitter end was so contradictory to the way he chose to behave under interrogation that there could be no reconciliation with personal honor. He had either to remain loyal to a friend and to a lost cause, or he had to atone to a sovereign he now considered legitimate. Perhaps, as can be seen in retrospect, he found a scrap of honor in the choice itself: a lesser person would have avoided the dilemma by all possible means, but he faced both the choice and its consequences.

III   *Bestuzhev and Ryleev's Death: New Evidence*

Bestuzhev's behavior during the investigation was thoroughly complex, and there is further evidence — some very unusual evidence — to support the view that Bestuzhev had a dilemma. It may very well have been that it was not he who decided to sacrifice his friend, but that Ryleev himself chose this course. It is a fact, for example, that in all of Bestuzhev's correspondence and other writing after 1825 he never, once gave so much as a hint of bad conscience. His letters from Siberia and the Caucasus contain numerous references to Ryleev's widow and children without revealing any feeling of dishonor toward them, and although his later literary works betray a great many doubts about the Decembrist affair, nothing in them can be construed as an indication of personal responsibility for Ryleev's death. Regrets over Ryleev's fate there were; personal blame there was not. The explanation of this curious situation is, perhaps, to be found in the ideals and personality of Ryleev. Ryleev clearly longed for martyrdom, and there is good reason to believe that Bestuzhev's post-revolt behavior followed Ryleev's intent.

Kondraty Ryleev was a literary and political idealist. His character allowed no compromise of beliefs. As Bestuzhev testified, Ryleev's ardent convictions enabled him to overwhelm his reluctant fellow Decembrists again and again. Unlike Bestuzhev, Ryleev had few doubts about his actions in the conspiracy and revolt, and in his testimony he spoke freely about his own role and about the general Decembrist ideals. He refused to say anything which would alleviate his own fate and he went to the gallows with a religious fervor.[27] As a matter of fact, he behaved precisely like the heroes of his historical poems: champions of the people who go gladly to their death in the knowledge that they have acted bravely for the good of their people and will be remembered in history as selfless martyrs in the cause of democracy.

Like Pushkin and many other poets of the Romantic period, Ryleev was fascinated by the ideal of the assassin's dagger, the death of tyrants, and especially the martyr's fate. But personal martyrdom was for him an actual, as well as a poetic, ideal; his poetry leaves little doubt that he desired to carry it into reality. It is always perilous to interpret art as a literal imitation of life, of course, but the similarity between Ryleev's fate and his heroes' is too close to be denied.

Ryleev's chief literary work is his historical verse tale *Voynarovsky* (1824), and it tells a great deal, perhaps all there is need to know, about his own and Bestuzhev's attitudes to the Decembrist dilemma. The work is, in fact, a fine example of life once again having the temerity to imitate art. Bestuzhev, for one, believed that the work was a dress rehearsal for the failure of the Decembrist conspiracy, a dramatization in advance of the dilemmas of both Ryleev and Bestuzhev as regards their reaction to the conflict between treason and a search for freedom. If his belief is correct, then it must be accepted that from the very outset both men knew how they would react to the revolt's failure.

Voynarovsky deals with the attempt of the Ukrainian Hetman Mazepa to gain his land's independence and freedom in 1709 by joining with the Swedes to wrest the Ukraine from the autocratic rule of Peter the Great. A basic theme is the struggle between democracy and autocracy, and Mazepa is interpreted as a revolutionary of total conviction, a leader willing to betray his loyalty to Peter in order to lead his people to freedom. The tale is narrated largely by the hero of the title, Voynarovsky, a young idealist who has many doubts about the justice of Mazepa's cause but is nonetheless willing to join his Hetman in treason. Voynarovsky tells his story in retrospect, from the point of view of a Siberian exile, an outcast reduced to an animal's existence as self-imposed punishment for his treason. While this narrative poem is mainly about Voynarovsky, not Mazepa, the ideals and dilemmas of both are clearly revealed, and it is equally evident that Voynarovsky is led to revolt through his admiration for Mazepa, his love for his country, and his desire for freedom. He loves Mazepa despite his awareness of his leader's penchant for intrigue, and is totally under the older man's influence.

Mazepa's ideals and attitudes are revealed in his own words. Early in the tale he forthrightly proclaims his faith in his conspiracy: "I revere the Great Peter; / But — bowing to fate — / Know then that I am his enemy from this day forth! . . ." He knows that his plan to win independence for his people is risky, but he has resolved to let fate decide "Whether glory awaits me, or disgrace." He is convinced that his cause is "The struggle of freedom with autocracy," and he carries out the revolt without doubts. After the revolt has failed, and Peter has proven victorious at the Battle of Poltava, Mazepa dies in regret and terror over the consequences of his rebellion: "I see the fearful Peter! / I hear his dreadful curses!" The ending of the tale suggests that the justness of a cause is best judged by the result.

Voynarovsky's attitudes — to both Mazepa and Peter — are equally explicit. He adores Mazepa and is prepared to support him to the end: " 'We revered in him the leader of the people, / We adored in him the father, / We loved in him the fatherland.' " At the same time, he never completely understands his secretive hero and suffers doubts about him: " 'I know not whether he really wished / To save the people of the Ukraine from misery.' " But whatever his doubts of the man, he also has complete faith in homeland and freedom:

> "I am prepared to endure any sacrifice,"
> I exclaimed, "for my native land;
> I will give even my children and my beloved wife,
> Saving only honor for myself."

And thus, despite his doubts, despite even his distrust of Mazepa's allies and fellow-conspirators, he devotes himself wholeheartedly to the conspiracy:

> "I gave myself to Mazepa blindly,
> And, friend of my fatherland, friend of virtue,
> I vowed terrible hostility
> Against Peter the Great.
> Akh, perhaps I was deluded,
> Overly hot from seething zeal;
> But in my blind hostility
> I deemed the Tsar a tyrant!"

And in the end, just as Mazepa reconciles himself with death, so Voynarovsky, convinced that " 'One instant destroyed / My native land forever,' " reconciles himself to his own harsh fate: " 'Alas, I shall die in this kingdom of darkness! / Thus have I been condemned by cruel fate.' "[28]

The tale only seems to credit Ryleev with a remarkable talent for prediction. The Decembrists knew very well, after all, that their conspiracy would lead them into an unavoidable confrontation with the government, and it did not require unusual foresight to anticipate failure against the powerful state. The elements of the respective attitudes and characters of Ryleev and Bestuzhev are thus in harmony with their literary representatives. Ryleev's fanatic idealism, his powerful personality, his love of intrigue, his determination to seek the freedom of the Russian people; Bestuzhev's doubts, his loyalty to Ryleev, his love for his country as measured against his duty to the Tsar. The tale indicates how much Ryleev was willing to sacrifice in the face of his pessimistic evaluation of the chances for success, and it shows that he sought martyrdom for himself while respecting Bestuzhev's different motivations. Both men understood one another in advance of the revolt and in their subsequent ordeal, both knew how the other planned to behave, and both took their different ways to December 14, 1825 and its aftermath. The crucial problem of their post-revolt behavior — their agreement that the one would place all the blame on the other — is clarified by one more piece of evidence.

In the late 1820's a young German scientist, Georg Adolph Erman, journeyed through Siberia on an expedition to measure the earth's magnetic field. There, in the settlement along the River Lena, he became friends with Bestuzhev. The two men worked together on Erman's project, and in his later essay, "Pismo k doctoru Ermanu" ("A Letter to Doctor Erman"), Bestuzhev expressed his gratitude to the German for an education in the natural sciences. Bestuzhev also confided his role in the Decembrist conspiracy to Erman and told him a story similar to the plot of Ryleev's *Voynarovsky*. In his own retelling of that story, Erman expressed Bestuzhev's view of the conspiracy, his role in it, and his thoughts about Ryleev's martyrdom. "Alexander Bestujev," Erman wrote, "had been engaged in the conspiracy long before the outbreak of the revolution." He had joined readily with "those who were for raising [the Russian people] on a sudden from servitude . . . [and] resolved on extreme measures. . . ." According to Bestuzhev, it was important that "they hoped to get the better subsequently of some of their associates who were strongly suspected of selfish ambition." When the revolt failed, Erman asserted, Bestuzhev underwent an immediate change of heart: "It is well known how the Emperor on that occasion, with a chivalrous contempt of death, awakened repentance in the more respectable of the insurgents and subdued the multitude. All felt as if proscribed by the moral power of the victory." Further, "the fetters which he [Bestuzhev] afterwards bore in the citadel of St. Petersburg and in one of the fortresses of Finland, nay, the deaths of his friends, who fell by his side, under the hands of the executioner on the scaffold, had never been able to efface from the exile's memory that one passage in the first night of his sufferings. He could not even today relate without shuddering how the Emperor came up to him . . . and with insupportable haughtiness of look told him of the loyalty of the deceased General Bestujev and the degeneracy of his son."[29]

If Erman's testimony is revealing of the profound effect the failure of the revolt had on Bestuzhev — an effect which Ryleev had anticipated in *Voynarovsky* — it reveals even more about his feelings over the fate of Ryleev and his own apparent ease of conscience. "But the poems of Ruileyev and Alexander Bestujev," Erman noted, "appear still more decidedly to have been not so much the consequence of a noble spirit crushed at its first opening as the tragic harbingers of the calamities about to ensue. They worked together for three years . . . until Ruileyev snatched for himself alone the gloomily bright crown of a prophet and unchanging friend." And Erman pointed deliberately to *Voynarovsky* as the key to the respective reactions of Ryleev and Bestuzhev. "The origin of this piece," he wrote, "can be explained only by supposing that, for some months before the poet's death, he knew, either from the sagacity of a sensitive and excited temper, or from a secret foreboding, how the threads of that web were to run, which he was assisting in the dark to weave. He beholds in spirit the dreams of the conspirators at an end, their plans wholly frustrated, their views stigmatized, his friend Bestujev expelled from society; he discerns beforehand every fine line and touch in the suffering of years, and finally, he sees himself in the hands of the executioner."

According to Erman, "Bestujev received in the prophetic poem the name of his predecessor in banishment. . . . His friend's fate was next to his heart, and Ruileyev therefore left his own image in the background; yet he often gives vent to the feeling of a conspirator who knows his own ignominious end and yet goes onwards."[30] Thus, it is likely that Ryleev's death was as much the result of his own desire for martyrdom as of Bestuzhev's dilemma, and that Bestuzhev may very well have promised Ryleev in advance to place the blame on him. In acting as they did, they could help alleviate the consequences for others while ensuring a niche in history for the surely doomed Ryleev. In reading Erman's retelling of Bestuzhev's account, it is not difficult to understand that the German scientist had been chosen as one means by which Ryleev's fate would become known.

IV   *After December: Siberia and the Caucasus*

Human behavior is seldom purely noble or purely ignominious, however, and none of what has just been said changes the fact that Bestuzhev's actions were partly opportunistic. His plea to be allowed to continue to serve his Tsar by saber or pen must be juxtaposed with the investigation committee's recommendation that his punishment be alleviated. He was the only literary Decembrist permitted to resume his career. As early as 1826, while still in prison, he was at work on a Romantic verse tale, *Andrei, kniaz pereiaslavskii* (Andrey, Prince of Pereyaslavl). During his period of exile, sympathetic friends such as Grech and Polevoy published as many of his previous works as they dared. He was able to put his Siberian exile to good use and wrote some of his finest poetry in the late 1820's. One winter he shaved his head bald to prevent himself from seeking company and used this interval to study several languages and literatures. It was not a pleasant time, and he was the victim of literary pirates,[31] but he continued to develop as a writer. And then, in 1830, first under the initials "A. M.," then under the pseudonym "Marlinsky," the ultra-Romantic prose tales which soon made *Marlinism* a byword in Russian began appearing in quick succession in leading journals. Written in a striking style and dealing as they did with exotic themes, it is little wonder that, as the pre-Revolutionary critic N. A. Kotlyarevsky put it, "the love of his readers was given to Marlinsky easily and quickly, despite his exceptional situation; his readers did not lag in their love for their anonymous teller of tales and they recognized Marlinsky's tales even without signature."[32]

For the next decade the Russian literary scene was dominated by the style of writing and living known as Marlinism. A quarter century after Marlinsky's death, Turgenev was to recall:

Marlinsky is out of fashion nowadays — no one reads him and his name is even sneered at; but in the thirties he thundered forth like no one else. He not only enjoyed the glory of the first prose writer in Russia, he even, which is more difficult and more rarely encountered, laid his imprint on the entire generation contemporary to him. Heroes *à la* Marlinsky were encountered everywhere, especially in the provinces and especially among army and artillery men. They conversed and corresponded in his language, in society they behaved gloomily — "with storms in their souls and fire in their blood."[33]

Young Russians began volunteering for military service in the Caucasus, Leo Tolstoy being perhaps the most famous of the hopeful *Kavkaztsy*. Budding writers began writing their own tales in the mode of Marlinism, and Marlinsky later became the hero of tales written in his own manner. Adolescents kissed the covers of books bearing the name Marlinsky, and later writers of the Caucasus, such as Lermontov and Tolstoy, responded or reacted to the Marlinsky manner. A series of authors of adventurous sea stories also made their appearance as imitators of Marlinsky, and horror stories were written in Marlinistic tones.

Despite the gap in time and obvious maturation between the tales of the early 1820's and those of the 1830's, it is quite apparent that the works of both periods are from one and the same writer. Yet, as far as the Russian public was concerned, there were two writers: The first was Alexander Bestuzhev — poet, critic, editor, translator, prose writer, and revolutionary; the second was Alexander Marlinsky, author of colorful and exciting Romantic prose tales. The Soviet Academician Mikhail P. Alekseev has examined the evidence relating to this situation and has rightly concluded: "It is necessary to realize that the metamorphosis of Bestuzhev into Marlinsky remained the secret of publishing and journalism circles. For the ordinary readers of the epoch, Bestuzhev disappeared forever from literature in 1826; to the readers of the new generation, who knew and loved Marlinsky, the name of Bestuzhev was unknown."[34] Thus, regardless of what name is used, it must be remembered that Bestuzhev preceded Marlinsky, and only later in the nineteenth century did the identity of the two become generally known.

Life in the Caucasus was not as desolate as in Siberia, but it was more dangerous. The scene of a fierce program for the pacification of the rebellious mountaineers, it was beset by even more fearful cholera epidemics. From the government's point of view, the Caucasus was an ideal place for the Decembrists and others to atone for their disloyalty or other imprudent acts. The Decembrist poet Prince Alexander I. Odoevsky died there, as did the poet Alexander I. Polezhaev, who was sent there for writing poetry in praise of the Decembrists. The poet Mikhail Lermontov was killed in a duel at a Caucasian spa during his second punitive tour of military duty there. Many of the minor Decembrists died there in bloody skirmishes and epidemics, and there was a general suspicion that the government assigned them the most perilous duties. This explains the ease with which Marlinsky obtained a transfer from Siberian exile and was able to join the army as a common soldier. He was shunted back and forth from skirmish to skirmish, battle to battle, quarantine to quarantine, humiliation to humiliation, and his time of public literary triumph soon became one of personal desperation.

He served in a death-hole fortress on the Caspian Sea, was kept in contact with the cholera epidemics that raged throughout the region, and found himself an easy victim of brutal, envious officers

who hoped to curry favor with the government by making his life
miserable. He participated in an especially large number of military
actions and brought more troubles upon himself by distinguishing
himself several times for bravery. Only on rare occasions did he
receive the medals or promotions for which he was recommended.
His health went into a steady decline, and his letters of the later
1830's are filled with complaints of illness. "I am in poor health,"
begins a typical letter to his younger brother Pavel, "I have constant
surges of blood to my head. . . ." "My health is better, dear Paul, but
I still have those surges to my head. . . . No one seeing me on my
return to Pyatigorsk would believe that I could keep up my military
duties, even in good weather — I have become that thin, pale,
sick. . . ."[35] In 1836 he wrote to Pavel:

> The one thing I pray for is that I might be given a corner where I could put
> down my staff and . . . serve Russian literature with my pen. It is evident
> they do not want this. Well, so be it! Driven as I am from region to region,
> never spending two months in one place, without quarters, without letters,
> without books, without newspapers, now exhausted by military duties, now
> half dead from illness — will I never be able to take a deep breath and cease
> to envy those who have done with their wanderings on this earth? And who
> will be worse off if I am a bit better off? Is it so difficult to throw a man a
> grain of happiness?[36]

In the 1830's two tragedies were added to Marlinsky's distress. In
1831 his younger brother Pyotr, who had endured almost six years of
systematic persecution for his involvement in the revolt on the day of
its execution (he was sixteen at the time), was seriously wounded in
battle. Under circumstances still not adequately explained, he was
driven insane by his brutal superiors and returned to his mother's
home in St. Petersburg, where he lived out his days in confinement
and mental terror.

A great many extravagant things have been written about the second tragedy, and even so authoritative a literary historian as Prince
Dmitry S. Mirsky has reported: "This incident left a profound scar
on his mind. He ceased writing and lost all interest in life."[37] In
reality, however profound the mark left on his mind, Marlinsky did
not cease writing; he was still active at the time of his death four
years later. During the winter of 1832-33 the city of Derbent underwent such a severe famine that it was beset by cannibalism.
Marlinsky kept a loaded pistol beneath his pillow. One evening,
Olga Nestertsova, the sixteen-year-old daughter of his landlady and,

according to rumors, his mistress, came to deliver his laundry. One of Marlinsky's friends was present, and all three were in a good mood. They began joking and laughing, and the girl ran around the room in high spirits. She hurled herself on Marlinsky's bed, and while "frisking" (her own term), the pistol fired through the pillow into her back. She died in agony fifty hours later. The nature of the accident was thought-provoking, to say the least, and the rumors it set loose were predictable. Even though the girl's death-bed confession, the friend's sworn testimony, a police investigation, and a military trial cleared Marlinsky, the rumor that he had murdered his mistress in a jealous rage grew into one more legend about the writer. Already the target of persecution, he was forced to endure a vile rumor campaign, and he was hard put to convince even his brother Pavel from believing what seemed obvious.[38] "I am unwell," Marlinsky wrote to Nikolay Grech just after the tragedy, "fate pursues me relentlessly, the calumny and spite of men haunt me — that is my news."[39]

Marlinsky's life in the Caucasus was not total misery, of course, nor was his love life always so tragic. His memoirist Ya. I. Kostenetsky maintained that "I am sure that on another stage of life, under different conditions, he would have become a true Don Juan." Thus, although Grech may have been correct in his belief that Marlinsky never forgot his unhappy love affair with Betancourt's daughter (the theme of unrequited love, unworthy woman, offended suitor is dominant in Marlinsky's writings), his love life seems to have been fairly strenuous.

According to Kostenetsky, Marlinsky was in love with a married woman in the Caucasus, a certain Alexandra Ivanovna N., who was once caught on her way to his quarters disguised in her husband's uniform. When the arresting officer tried to blackmail her into submitting to him, Marlinsky swore to silence the man "Caucasian fashion," and the officer quickly obtained a transfer. Kostenetsky has also testified that "It happened more than once that, in the night, with dagger in hand, he would creep stealthily along the Derbent wall and over the flat roofs of houses to some young Persian girl awaiting him with impatience."[40] Kostenetsky seems to have been an exaggerator, and he even admits candidly to stealing his hero's love letters,[41] but Marlinsky's own testimony, in a letter to Pavel in 1832, would seem to support him: "And stealing through the night, along the walls, through windows, in danger of breaking my neck, or of having to lay someone low; always with my dagger at the ready and my ear on the clock . . . and her disguising of herself, and the strolls, and visits to my place . . . and the successful and amusing deceptions of the Argusses — oh! I am a most fascinating novel in the vein of Faublas!"[42]

Moreover, despite the lack of peace and privacy, Marlinsky's was a productive life. Between 1830 and 1836 he wrote his best and most lengthy prose tales — fifteen in all — to which he added his major essay on Romanticism, a handful of other essays, long and short, the ten travel essays on the Caucasus, and an unknown number of articles, anecdotes, newspaper reports, and battle accounts of the Caucasus. He wrote some of his finest folk poems and songs and translated many others in the years from 1830 to the year of his death in 1837. He wrote a still unpublished account of the famous bandit Mulla Nur and he began writing a grammar of the Tatar language. Beginning in 1835 he wrote the four chapters of the unfinished novel *Vadimov*. He wrote accounts of the uprising of Kaza-Mulla in the early 1830's and published them in the newspaper *Severnaya pchela (The Northern Bee)*. He maintained a voluminous correspondence with various members of his family, far off in Siberia or in St. Petersburg, and kept up an equally large correspondence, for business and friendship's sake, with the Polevoy brothers, Faddey Bulgarin, Nikolay Grech, and many other publishers and editors. He was kept busy with official correspondence, either to win back his officer's rank, or to secure a promised medal for numerous acts of bravery, or to gain release from arduous and unwarranted duty assignments. He mastered the chief dialects of the Caucasus and established himself as a still-recognized authority on the area. When one realizes how he was shunted from place to place, hindered, even tormented for the last seven years of his life, and that he was still able to function as a productive man of letters, then there can be no stinting of admiration for him.

By 1836, however, Marlinsky could no longer avoid the fact that there was a pattern to his misery. He strove to conduct himself as a loyal soldier and to exhibit his loyalty to Nicholas I, but could not refrain from complaining about the treatment which led him to his death in 1837. As early as 1831 he complained in a letter to Nikolay Polevoy: "The terrible situation of my brother Pyotr, seriously wounded in the arm, rends me a hundred times more than my own incredible existence, which is vulnerable to any scoundrel. Would you believe that here in the land of vineyards and olives I long for Yakutsk! And little wonder — there I was at least independent, but here!!!" He was especially vulnerable to literary pirates, and in an 1833 letter to Ksenofont Polevoy, requesting help with a complaint against the publisher Smirdin, he raged: "The villain! How dare he toy with me? Or did he think . . . to buy my word and my silence with money? Money! When I would not even use hypocrisy to buy my freedom, the first and only joy and desire of my soul. . . ." In one of his first complaints over lack of permanence he wrote to his brothers in Siberia, also in 1833: "I am presently unwell and for all that I am spending only a few days in Derbent, for I have been transferred . . . to Akhaltsykh. If it were up to me, I would refuse; there is nothing I care for in Georgia, and the graveyard here is just as peaceful as anywhere else; but I am going." In 1836 he was transferred to one of the most disease-ridden posts in the Caucasus and wrote a letter to Count Alexander Kh. Benckendorf, the Tsar's minister and secret police chief, to plead for a reassignment, even stooping in one instance to beg: "Before God and the world I make bold to say, Most Radiant Count, that repentance has long ago made a new man of me and convinced me in my soul that in all the time which has passed since 1826, I have not been guilty toward the Tsar of a single misbehavior, neither in word, nor in thought; that I have served him as befits a valiant soldier; that I have endured much, suffered much. . . ."[43]

Marlinsky's death was as violent, tragic, and mysterious as his life, and there is considerable evidence that he intended it to be that way. In both his literary works and his correspondence of the last years he took a great interest in "Byronic" deaths, and he expressed envy of the English poet's "glamorous" death in the Greek revolution. Two of his works written in the years just prior to his death — *On byl ubit* ("He Was Killed") and the chapter titled "Zhurnal Vadimova" ("Vadimov's Journal") of the uncompleted novel *Vadimov* — are based on the thoughts of men preparing for their own deaths. Marlinsky's brother Mikhail testified in regard to the news of his death that "we were already prepared for it, both by his letters filled with his determination to seek death and by the already visible intentions of the government to bring him to account."[44] In a letter to Pavel of February 23, 1837, just three months before his death, Marlinsky did indeed seem to be preparing for a romantic dénouement. Relating how he had services held for the other two literary Alexanders — Pushkin just killed in a duel and Griboedov hacked to pieces by a mob in Teheran — he declared with great dramatism: "I cried then as I am crying now, with hot tears, cried for a friend and a comrade in arms, cried for myself; and when the priest chanted, 'Za ubiennykh bolyar Aleksandra i Aleksandra,' my sobs tore at my breast — the phrase seemed to me to be not only a remembrance, but also a premonition. . . . Yes, I sense that my death will be just as violent and unexpected, that it is already close at hand. . . ."[45]

On June 7, 1837 a Russian pacification force landed at Cape Adler on the Caspian Sea and attacked a band of mountaineers. One segment of the Russian picket line, positioned in a wooded area, advanced ahead of the main line and was cut off. As he had done on several recent occasions, Marlinsky insisted that he be allowed to deliver the order to fall back, and he arrived just in time to be cut off with the others. In the heat of battle he was seen to run forward into some bushes; a few minutes later he was dragged back wounded. He was last seen leaning against a tree, bleeding heavily from a chest wound. His body was never found, and it was believed he had been hacked to pieces.

If, as has been claimed, Marlinsky had planned his own death, he could not have succeeded better; rumors grew into legends, and the legends led to literary tales and hot debates in the newspapers and journals. It was said that he had planned his own death to end the government's persecutions and to crown an already notorious reputation. It was said that his death was not self-intended, but deliberate murder by government decree. It was said that his wounds had been light and that he had used his reputation among the mountaineers to evade the government and live out a life in peace, and some even believed he had arranged the whole event to cover an escape. One story had it that he had joined the Circassians and had become a rebel leader; another reported he had joined Mulla Nur's famous robber band; still another explained he had fallen in love with a beautiful girl of the mountains — just like his own heroes — and lived out an idyllic life in hiding. He was said to have escaped to Persia, and even to have become a writer in some other country. One man claimed to have met him in the mountains many years later, living happily with five wives. All of these legends — even the most implausible — have been suggested by bits and pieces of tantalizing evidence in his letters and prose tales.[46]

Although Marlinsky dominated the literary decade of the 1830's, his fame was soon overshadowed by his greater contemporaries, and his literary manner was quickly superseded by the greater sophistication of the Russian Realists. As is so often the case, the reasons for his unprecedented popularity are also the source of his quick descent to a lesser literary appreciation. N. A. Kotlyarevsky seems to have realized this perfectly when he wrote that "the impressionability of his brisk mind, the agitations of his soul, the fluctuation of his moods, and, finally, the quick pace of his speech — free, brilliant and unstinting of metaphors — are the source of all his merits as a writer and of his shortcomings."[47] A time soon came when he, the writer so closely identified with Romanticism, was eclipsed along with the Romantic period, and he seemed to the Realists to be a stereotype of what they disliked about Romantic creativity. As early as 1834 the critic Belinsky had begun a campaign to bring Marlinsky down from the heights of his popularity. Within decades after his death, as Turgenev noted, "his name was even sneered at."

Nevertheless, even Belinsky admitted that "Mr. Marlinsky's prose tales . . . achieved much of benefit for Russian literature, and were a great step forward for it."[48] Marlinsky should be seen, then, as a standard bearer of his age, as a man of letters whose contributions to Russian literature are far more revealing of the quality and the nature of his literary period than those of the men who lent their names to the time. If this is a modest role in the history of a literature, it remains a significant one, and there is much to be appreciated in his life and works.

CHAPTER 2

Bestuzhev the Critic

BESTUZHEV the Critic (to borrow a favored Russian
title) has been accorded a very prominent position in
the history of Russian criticism, and his contributions to his country's
letters have been closely defined by Soviet scholars. Together with
his friend Kondraty Ryleev he is considered a chief representative of
the Decembrist or Civic trend within the Romantic movement, and
thus a founder of the frequently dominant tradition of sociopolitical
literary criticism. The importance of this position should not be un-
derestimated, for it signifies that Bestuzhev is honored as the intellectual ancestor of such major critics and philosophers as Belinsky,
Herzen, Nekrasov, Chernyshevsky, and Dobrolyubov. He is no less
than a pioneer of the cultural trend that leads to the Civicism of the
later nineteenth century and to Positivism, Utilitarianism, Nihilism,
Populism, and Socialist Realism. For this reason the three politically
oriented "Glances" at Russian literature which prefaced the annual
issues of *The Polar Star* and served as its editorial manifesto are
treated as Bestuzhev's central contribution to Romantic criticism.
They have been thoroughly gleaned for their proclamations of
Decembrist ideology.[1]

Nor can Bestuzhev's importance as a Civic-Decembrist critic be
denied. His critical works do indeed contain political statements,
and his critical activities, especially his co-editorship of *The Polar
Star*, were coordinated with his activities as a political conspirator.
But the Civic-Decembrist trend does not define the limits of his contributions; his political interests almost always are subordinated in
his writings to literary considerations. It might even be argued that
Civicism occupies a relatively minor position in the totality of his
critical writings, and his literary contributions have been too often
assigned a secondary importance by overly exclusive political interpretations. He was very much a language-oriented critic, for exam-

ple, and his articles are remarkable for the detailed care with which he devoted himself to formal, linguistic, and stylistic analyses. Languages, especially the Russian language, were his specialty as a critic — the most basic and explicitly stated assumption of his literary judgments. Given the fact that the reform of the Russian language and the modernization of the standard literary language were among the most important problems of Russian literature during the Romantic period, it can even be argued that his concern with language and style, not his Civicism, gained him his deserved prominence in Russian literature; all the more so, in that the Russian language was in its turn the basis of the chief problem facing the Russian Romantics: the development of Russia's first national literature of world importance.

Consequently, while there is no need for a reassessment of Bestuzhev's Civic position, there is great need for an examination of several other contributions which may be understood as the main outlines of his career as a Romantic critic. These contributions, each of which was built on the others in chronological succession, are: a debate in the early 1820's with the critic Pavel A. Katenin which resulted in the overthrow of erroneous views of the origin and nature of the Russian language and in the establishment of respect for the language and literary reforms begun by the Sentimentalist writer N. M. Karamzin; a demonstration of the liabilities of Neoclassical principles in the development of a modern national literature and the transformation of this question into a theoretically sound Romantic interpretation of the all-important Russian concept of *narodnost'*; an attempt to assert the legitimacy of the "modern school" in Russia by emphasizing the continuity between ancient and modern Russian literature; a significant contribution to the development of Russian literary criticism by translating a number of the most important European Romantic critical works into Russian; and the culmination of Bestuzhev's career in 1833 with an essay on the theory of Romanticism and history, a work in which he completed his attempts to apply European Romantic theory to Russian conditions.

I   *The Modernization of the Russian Literary Language*

The talents which most immediately define Bestuzhev the critic are his sharp wit, his love of polemics, and his ability to deal effectively with nuances of language and style. He began his career as a translator in 1818 with the publication of a German treatise on Baltic history and in 1819 he established himself as a book reviewer. He made his reputation as a critic in 1819 with two sharp attacks on dramatic works by Prince Alexander Shakhovskoy and Pavel Katenin, and the audacity with which he undertook to criticize these two powerful literary figures made him a critic with whom to contend for the next six years. In 1820 he published his first translation of a European critical work, and this inaugurates his extensive work as a translator who introduces Western literary standards into Russia. During the next several years he published some twenty translations of critical statements by such Europeans as Blair, Jomar, Robertson, Bacon, Artaud, Weiss, Schiller, Sulzer, and Wordsworth. Between 1819 and late 1822 Bestuzhev wrote over thirty articles, essays, analyses, critiques, reviews, and letters to the editor, and he was a regular contributor to such influential journals as *Syn otechestva* ("Son of the Fatherland"), *Sorevnovatel' prosveshcheniyai blagotvoreniya* ("The Champion of Enlightenment and Philanthropy"), and *Blagonamerenny* ("The Well-Intentioned"). He involved himself in virtually every literary controversy of the time. In 1821 he debated with Orest Somov the question of Vasily A. Zhukovsky's translation of Schiller's ballad *Der Fischer* and he debated a wide variety of other subjects with such leading critics as Katenin, Bulgarin, Grech, Vyazemsky, Küchelbecker, and Shishkov. From 1823 through 1825 his efforts as a critic were devoted to the publication of *The Polar Star*, his three essays enabling him to exert influence on Russian literature during these crucial years in the development of the Romantic movement. He and Ryleev also undertook such important literary ventures as the editing of Baratynsky's first collected poems and negotiated the rights to Pushkin's *Eugene Onegin*. The failure of the revolt of December 14, 1825 brought a halt to Bestuzhev's career as a critic, but in 1827 he wrote an unpublished treatise "O romantizme" ("On Romanticism") which has since been recognized as an important statement, and in 1833, under the name Marlinsky, he was able to publish his major essay, written *à propos* of Polevoy's novel, and secure a reputation as a respectable Romantic literary theorist.[2]

If Bestuzhev's objective in attacking Shakhovskoy and Katenin in 1819 was literary sensationalism, he could not have made a more brilliant choice of targets. Both men had already been identified as literary "old believers;" somewhat pompous by personality, they had wielded their influence in ways guaranteed to bring unpopularity. By attacking Shakhovskoy, Bestuzhev could take direct aim at an immediately identifiable Neoclassicist, an ally of the literary and linguistic reactionary Admiral Shiskov, and an opponent of the so-called Karamzinians. By attacking Katenin, he could make him a target as the leader of a more conservative Romantic grouping, the so-called Katenin circle, and a man who was a partial ally of the Shishkov camp and a total enemy of the Karamzinian reforms. Of the two targets, Katenin turned out to be the most important, for Bestuzhev's initial attack quickly became a campaign which propelled him into the midst of the controversy over the modernization of the Russian language.

Pavel Katenin was perhaps the first Romantic in Russia, but he was also a contrary person: when Romanticism began to become fashionable, he proclaimed himself a Neoclassicist. In 1815 he set off one of the first major Romantic polemics over literary form and style with his free translation of Bürger's folk ballad *Lenore*, under the title *Olga*. His translation was intended to be a challenge to Zhukovsky's 1808 translation of the same ballad under the title *Lyudmila*. In the ensuing polemic, conducted by the poet and translator Nikolay I. Gnedich and Katenin's young admirer Alexander S. Griboedov, lines were drawn between the Karamzinians and the small circle which became known as the Kateninites. In the opinion of Griboedov, the language of the Karamzinians was too "affected," too "Frenchified," and too much in the manner of melancholy German Romantic poetry. In their turn, the Karamzinians were offended by the "common-folk vulgarity" of Katenin's style; they were dubious about his use of the lexicon and syntax of Russian folk songs and considered the use of this "low" colloquial standard to be a violation of Karamzin's preference for the language of the educated elite in literary works. According to Gnedich, Zhukovsky's translation was superior because it was more native to Russian conditions than Katenin's.[3] In the next several years after 1815 Katenin continued to write what he believed were true folk ballads, and his style, coupled with vocal support for Shishkov's contention that Russian is descended directly from Old Slavic, enabled him to establish a minority Romantic position in opposition to the Karamzinians. His position differed from that of the Shishkovites in that he was not a political conservative. His basic assumptions were not really Neoclassical; he had no interest in Bible mysticism; and although he deplored *calques* — a key point of Shishkovite-Karamzinian contention — he was an erudite admirer of French, Spanish, and Italian literatures.[4]

Bestuzhev's criticisms of Katenin, specifically his translation of

Racine's drama *Esther*, were based on two points: it was a bad translation and its lexicon contained too many Old Slavic words. For these reasons the work is "an almost unbroken chain of unforgivable errors in taste, meaning, and most often language, to say nothing of the demands of poetry and harmony." Bestuzhev listed word after word he considered offensive to good diction and out of keeping with modern Russian style. He especially disliked Katenin's metaphors and noted sarcastically that "reading this translation is like seeing oneself in masquerade, for everything in it sings and dances. . . . "[5] Cruelly ridiculing both translation and translator, he seems to have been intent on establishing himself as a David out to get Goliath. Yet despite his fondness for his own sharp wit, his article is a sound piece of criticism and his linguistic knowledge is evident. His objections are inevitably to "low" or colloquial words and to Katenin's profusion of Old Slavic words taken from Biblical sources. Both objections are firmly in the realm of Karamzinian esthetics, and this helped to identify him at the very start of his career as a continuator of the Karamzinian reforms.

Soon Bestuzhev resumed his campaign against Katenin. In an 1820 review of current literature, a second member of the Katenin circle, Wilhelm K. Küchelbecker, turned his attention to the ballads of Zhukovsky and Katenin, praising the latter for his "attempt to unite our un-Russian poetry with the rich poetry of Russian native songs, fairy tales, and legends — with the poetry of Russian mores and customs." In Küchelbecker's opinion, Katenin was the only true Romantic in Russia.[6] Bestuzhev disagreed. In a "Letter to the Editor" of the journal *Son of the Fatherland* he turned his invective on Katenin's historical ballad *Mstislav Mstislavich*, criticizing it for its mixture of "common *narodnost'* " with what he jeeringly called *slavianshchina*, and even accusing Katenin of "lack of *narodnost'*. " The accusations were serious, for not only was *narodnost'* — national self-sufficiency — the most highly prized literary quality of Russians concerned with creating their own national literature from native sources, but it was so crucial to Russian Romanticism as to be all but synonymous with the movement. It was the keystone to the Kateninite "folk" position and the crux of the 1815 battle of the ballad.

In Bestuzhev's view, Katenin's lack of *narodnost'* could be attributed to his *slavianshchina* — his Shishkov-oriented preference for Old Slavic words. He again listed numerous examples taken from the Old Slavic lexicon and concluded with a jeer: "In a word, this work, written without aim, beginning, or end, without the coloring of the time and without the flowers (I will not say 'mushrooms') of modern literature . . . obliges one to involuntarily repeat the famous words — that it is more difficult to express one's opinion of it than it was to write it."[7] One month later, in a "Letter to the Editor" of *The Well-Intentioned*, Bestuzhev (using his pseudonym Marlinsky for the first time) turned his attention to Katenin's translation of Racine's *Athalie* under the title *Athalie's Dream;* here he stated explicitly that Katenin's lexicon was too archaic to be tolerated. Listing and analyzing examples of archaisms, he asserted that modern literature has no place for such a profusion of Old Slavic words and phrases. To the glee of his readers, he proposed to build a "literary *Kunstkamera*" (the museum in St. Petersburg where Peter the Great kept his pickled freaks) and referred to his list of archaisms as Katenin's "freaks of language."[8]

In 1822 Bestuzhev again attacked Katenin, this time in the context of a wide-ranging debate over Romanticism provoked by Grech's *Attempt at a Brief History of Russian Literature*. He now enlarged the scope of the debate to encompass other questions of the modernization of the Russian literary language. Nikolay I. Grech was prominent in literary circles as a philologist, pedagogue, critic, and publisher of *Son of the Fatherland*. His *Brief History* is not important in the history of Russian letters, but at the time of its appearance in 1822 it was highly controversial, particularly for its covert defense of a literary position already known as "the new, the modern, the so-called Romantic school." Grech's basic assumption about the history of a national literature was that the degree of a nation's enlightenment is indicated by its language and literature. Literature is based on language, either "the language of the people" or "the language of books." He divided the history of Russian literature into ancient and modern periods (the established Romantic Idealist contrast), subdividing the modern (post-Petrine) period into three literary generations: the Lomonosovian, the Karamzinian, and the generation since Karamzin.[9] This tri-generation schema espoused by many critics of the 1820's was central to their attempts to sort out the events of their nation's literary history. The eighteenth-century scholar, scientist, grammarian, and poet Mikhailo V. Lomonosov was generally identified as a founder of Russian Neoclassicism, Karamzin was considered the precursor of Russian Romanticism, and "the generation since Karamzin" was a commonly used euphemism for Romanticism.[10]

The basis of Lomonosov's language and literary reforms had been the establishment of five language levels based on vocabulary and used on three style levels — High, Middle, and Low. This schema was fitted to a hierarchy of literary genres similar to the Neoclassical system promulgated by Boileau in *L'art poétique.* Lomonosov placed a high value on Old Church Slavonic and helped systematize the Russian literary language by recommending principles for the adoption of foreign words and syntax. A serious defect of his reforms was the fact that he based Russian grammar on German and Latin syntax, thus introducing a partial reason for the awkwardness of the eighteenth-century literary language. But ultimately the Lomonosov reforms were an important step forward in the modernization of the Russian language and literature, and they survived the eighteenth century, despite a steady trend toward eventual breakdown.[11]

In their turn, the Karamzin reforms were based on extensive modifications of the Lomonosov model: the elimination of the German, Latin, and other awkward syntactical elements, a rejection of Old Church Slavonic in literary works, and a discarding of archaic lexical items at the extremes of the High and Low levels. In effect, a primarily Middle level corresponding to the language of the educated elite was established for literary works, while the Low colloquial level came to be considered unfit for literature. As a solution to the problem of foreign adoptions, Karamzin recommended the European literary languages, especially the French language, as models for a Russian literary standard. The defects of the Karamzinian reforms were two. First, the language of the cultured elite (the Kateninites referred to it contemptuously as "the language of the salon") was highly Frenchified, and this ran counter to Karamzin's own belief in the superiority of the "born-to-the-soil" Russian language. And second, the Karamzinian contempt for colloquial language created a schism between the spoken and literary languages and hindered poets from cultivating the folk sources which Romantic esthetics made important to Russians.[12]

Karamzin's fiercest opponent was Admiral Shishkov, who considered *calques* to be linguistically pernicious, if not politically subversive. He insisted that modern Russian was descended directly from Old Slavic and was thus the only pure Slavic language. Although the Shishkovites were generally Neoclassicists, and thus under the influence of French culture, they looked back to the Lomonosov reforms for their roots and were determined to protect their native language from the "Frenchified" Karamzinian reforms.[13] During the early nineteenth century the Shishkovites were powerful, but by the early 1820's they were considerd antiquated, and the Katenites took over the privilege — or stigma — of keepers of *Slavianshchina*. The significance of the Bestuzhev-Katenin confrontation, then, is that it became a full-fledged Romantic clash over problems that had been plaguing Russians for almost a century and were still in need of solutions that were crucial to the development of a national literature.

To Katenin, Grech's *Brief History* was a fine opportunity to express the essentials of his views of the Russian language. All the more so in that Grech's delineation of a language of books and a language of the people might have seemed to vindicate his own objections to the schism between the spoken and written language standards. In all other respects, however, Grech supported the Karamzinian reforms, and Katenin thought he detected a lack of respect for the Lomonosov reforms. Turning to Grech's remarks on the language of books, he asked in a "Letter to the Editor" of *Son of the Fatherland:* ". . . in what ancient book do you find an outright Russian language?" In his view, the Old Slavic language had been destroyed by the Tatar influence and had ceased to exist until it was revived by Lomonosov, who "made it into exactly what it is today . . . by adhering to a language both Slavic and Church." That is, Lomonosov's reforms had been no less than a creation of a modern Russian language by restoring the Old Slavic language in all its purity. By implication, the Karamzinian diction was false, the Kateninite diction — based as it was on Old Slavic — correct. Then, placing himself squarely in favor of the Lomonosov reforms as the only true direction for the Russian language to take, Katenin pleaded: "Must we stray from the path so fortuitously marked out [by Lomonosov]? is it not better to follow his lead and with renewed efforts appropriate for ourselves new riches lying hidden in our born-to-the-soil language? . . . I know of all the jeers of the modern school about Slavonophiles, Varango-Rossen, and such; but I make so bold as to inquire of these ridiculers, in just what language are we to write the épopée, the tragedy, or even serious, genteel prose? . . ."[14]

Bestuzhev's reply was immediate, and he took the occasion to reject the Old Slavic-modern Russian equation. In an article he had just published, a critique of Grech's *Brief History*, Bestuzhev also had objected to Grech's failure to account for a Church language,[15] but now he was more interested in striking another blow against Katenin. In an article titled "Remarks on Criticisms Concerning *An*

Attempt at a Brief History of Russian Literature," he discussed the *slavianshchina* at length, pointing out that it had long since been proved that Russian was not a direct descendant of Old Slavic and that the Lomonosov reforms were based on a high evaluation of Old Church Slavonic as a literary language, rather than a restoration of the tribal dialects known as Old Slavic. And then, turning to the matter of prescribed generic-stylistic hierarchies, he made it clear that he objected not to the use of Old Slavic words in modern literary works, but rather to the extent of their use. "The [Old] Slavic language serves us nowadays as an arsenal," he asserted, "we take from it *sword* and *helmet* but we no longer array our heroes in *ox-hides* beneath their *chainmail,* and we dress ourselves in *caftans* only for masquerades. For that matter, I would prefer for the sake of rarity that a poem or tragedy written in our time in the [Old] Slavic language be not in verse, but in noble (that is, not merchant) prose."[16]

The two positions are thus clear. To Katenin, the Lomonosov reforms were both correct and viable, and his plea for their preservation was linked with his support of the Shishkovite Old Slavic-modern Russian equation. He was therefore opposed to the Karamzinian reforms, not because he was ethnocentrically concerned with the harmful effects of *calques,* but because he believed that the true Russian language was vastly superior in its ancient sources to any foreign model. Like Shishkov and other Neoclassicists, he wanted to preserve Lomonosov's hierarchy of genres and styles. To Bestuzhev, on the other hand, the Kateninite position was unacceptable. He was on solid ground in challenging Katenin's exaggerated claims for the Lomonosov reforms, and Katenin's insistence on the Shishkovite equation, which was false, enabled him to undercut the Kateninite position on the origin and nature of the Russian language. Above all, he could not tolerate Katenin's plea for the preservation of Lomonosov's hierarchy. In his view, it was permissible to use Old Slavic words in moderation, for stylistic effect, but not as the fundamental basis of the modern literary language, and not in accordance with stylistic-generic prescriptions. In substantiation of this opinion, he pointed out that young Pushkin and the two most prominent Karamzinians, Vasily Zhukovsky and Konstantin N. Batyushkov, all used Old Slavic words in "light" and "erotic" verse.[17] He undoubtedly had his own style in mind here, for he regularly used words of Old Slavic origin to impart temporal and local color to his historical prose tales. In his view, this was a stylistically correct usage, and this is the significance of his earlier charge that Katenin had failed to achieve either the "coloring of the time" or the equality of modern literature in his historical ballads.

II Romanticism, Neoclassicism, and The Polar Star

The Bestuzhev-Katenin portion of the general debate over Grech's *Brief History* marks the end of the *slavianshchina* as a credible literary position, but it was only the beginning of Bestuzhev's attempt to propagate a more sound view of the Russian language and its use in modern literary works. Bestuzhev was not the originator of his ideas, for he was simply utilizing the knowledge already made known by philologists; and he cannot take sole credit for the focus of attention on the erroneous assumptions of the Shishkovites and Kateninites, for other critics were equally active in the campaign to discredit the *slavianshchina*. But more than any other critic, Bestuzhev devoted himself fully to the language problem and to the language-oriented analyses of style that were his specialty.

He had not yet revealed the essentials of his own view of the Russian language, however, and he turned to this task in the first annual issue of *The Polar Star*, in the article titled "Vzglyad na staruyu i novuyu slovesnost' v Rossii" ("A Glance at Ancient and Modern Literature in Russia," 1823). In his view, Old Russian was a mixture of the language of the "Varango-Rossen" (the Varangians or Normans who came to ancient *Rus* in the eleventh century) with the "native language" of some of the Slavic tribes, and this separation from Old Slavic had been consolidated by the influence of Greek via the Gospels. In apparent response to Katenin's assertion that Russian was the original Old Slavic language ruined by the Tatars and restored by Lomonosov, Bestuzhev insisted that "the reign of the Tatars left scarcely perceptible traces" in the Russian language and that Russian had been far more seriously damaged by the influence of Polish in the sixteenth and seventeenth centuries, the Germanisms and Latinisms which had crept in during the reign of Peter the Great (he made no mention of Lomonosov here), and the Gallicisms which had been inundating the language ever since the reign of Elizabeth I in the early eighteenth century. These alien influences had modified, in fact debased, the Russian language. By implication, one of the tasks of the modernization of the Russian language should be to rid it of unnatural adoptions.[18]

Although Bestuzhev's stress on the influence of the Scandinavians (the well-known Varangian theory) is subject to doubt today, his knowledge of the origin of the Russian language is otherwise sound. It is true that the Tatar influence was not so serious as Katenin claimed, and the influences of Polish, Latin, German, and French, to say nothing of the Greek of the Bible, are in keeping with Bestuzhev's chronology. He was interested in more than the past history of the language, however, and at this time he began to transform his concern for the modern literary language, specifically his disapproval of Gallicisms, into an attack on Neoclassicism. He began his second article, "Vzglyad na russkuyu slovesnost' v techenie 1823 goda" ("A Glance at Russian Literature in the Course of 1823," 1824) with a praise of the year 1812 when "the words 'fatherland' and 'glory' electrified everyone." Unfortunately, after the war "a hidden passion for Gallicisms suddenly seized all positions with more strength than before," and thus the French language had proved victorious where the French army failed.[19]

In his expression of distaste for French *calques* and his stress on patriotism, Bestuzhev was in no way supporting either the Shishkovite or the Kateninite positions, and his remarks are well in keeping with Karamzinian esthetics. His objection was not to the use of French as a model for Russian, but to the extent — and even more — to the nature of that use. His objections were to servile imitation of foreign models without concern for the native condition of the Russian language, and he made these objections even more clear in his third article, "Vzglyad na russkuyu slovesnost' v techenie 1824 i nachale 1825 godov" ("A Glance at Russian Literature in the Course of 1824 and the Beginning of 1825," 1825). In doing so, he also revealed that his true target was French Neoclassicism.

Putting forth the notion that the "literature of all peoples . . . begins with an age of genius" and this is followed by "an age of mediocrity, awe, and analysis," or an age of criticism, Bestuzhev maintained that in Russia the age of criticism had already begun, but there had been no age of genius. The reason for this reversal of the rule of development of a national literature, Bestuzhev believed, was evident: ". . . we have been raised by foreigners. We have suckled with our mothers' milk a lack of *narodnost'* and an awe only for what is alien. . . ." Moreover, "to crown our misfortune, we have been raised exclusively on French literature, which is not at all suitable for the nature of the Russian people or the spirit of the Russian language." Russia's tragedy was that it had opened itself to the West at just the time when French

Neoclassicism dominated Europe. Russia had as a consequence gone directly to the age of criticism under the influence of "that time of polemical tittle-tattle. . . ."[20] Russia had learned to imitate, rather than create. The national originality of the Russian language and literature had thus been harmed by servility, imitation, and slavery to French Neoclassical principles.

Bestuzhev did not say more than this, but he left no doubt that unless Russia rid itself of Neoclassicism it would not be able to develop its own national literature. He did not use the word Romanticism, but his use of the term *narodnost'* is in perfect keeping with the Romantic assumption that a national literature can preserve its independence only so long as a response to foreign influences does not become mere imitation and when native features are treated as a national literature's prime source of inspiration. Bestuzhev's use of the word therefore reveals the start of his attempt to relate the problem of language to this key Russian concept and to base this relationship firmly on European Romantic theory.

Because the very meaning of *narodnost'* is so closely bound up with indigenousness, it has not always been appreciated how thoroughly the Russian Romantics relied on European intellectual sources for articulated definitions of the problem.[21] Virtually every Russian of the 1820's who concerned himself with *narodnost'* turned to European Romantic theory, especially Romantic Idealism, for guidance. Their search led them directly to the chief founders of the European concept of national originality — Johann Gottfried Herder, Friedrich and August Schlegel, Madame de Staël, Sismondi, and Johann Peter Friedrich Ancillon. This is also true of Bestuzhev, and in his theory of the two ages of national development his interest in European Romantic theory is most clearly revealed.

Both the theory and Bestuzhev's phrasing of it are taken from Jean Charles Léonard Simonde de Sismondi's *De la littérature du midi de l'Europe* (1813; rev. 1817). Chapters of the book had recently been published in Russian journals, and Sismondi's authority in Russia was great. In Sismondi's view, "at the period when nations, yet in their infancy, are animated by a creative genius, which endows them with a poetry of their own . . . the literature of other nations is unknown to them. . . ." This had been the case with every nation which "had not suffered the spirit of imitation to extinguish its natural vigor." But the age of genius is succeeded by an age in which "reflection soon succeeds to this vehement effervescence, self-examination takes place . . . the spirit of analysis chills the imagination and the heart. . . ." In this new age "the mind is no longer ignorant of itself . . . everything is a matter of observation . . . everything is governed by rules . . . refinement of intellect has gained the superiority over mere native talent."[22]

Not all of Bestuzhev's contemporaries agreed with his adroit reversal of Sismondi's theory of national development,[23] but his application of the theory to Russian conditions was central to the controversy over *narodnost'*. The Romantics of the 1820's, who had been awakened to the Romantic ideals of imagination and originality, were anxious over the impact that had been made on their literature by the Neoclassical principle of imitation as the chief source of creativity. All the more so since they were painfully conscious that the foundations which had been laid for their literature in the eighteenth century were far too dependent on European cultural values. Those European Romantic theorists who had verbalized the concept of national originality were therefore important to the Russians, because they not only taught that an independent native language is the very basis of an original national literature, but they demonstrated that the only nations that need fear alien influences are those that *imitate* rather than assimilate.

Thus, the concept of national originality provided a justification for continued Russian interest in European values and a formula for adopting foreign values without harming indigenous institutions. Above all, those theorists who, like Sismondi, stressed the superiority of young and vigorous nations were a godsend to the Russians, anxious as they were about Russia's relative lack of sophistication and their need to lay the foundation for an original national literature. The concept provided tailor-made answers to the problem of Russia and the West, and thus it became a basis for the concept of *narodnost'*. For Bestuzhev, then, Sismondi's theory was perfectly suited for adaptation to the Russian historical experience, and it caused him great anxiety that French Neoclassicism might have "suffered the spirit of imitation to extinguish [Russia's] natural vigor." This is the meaning of his fear that Russians had been "raised exclusively on French literature."

As it happens, Sismondi's theory is itself a new application of the traditional division of world literature into ancient and modern periods, and an adaptation of that division as it was defined, in Romantic terms, by August and Friedrich Schlegel. The ancient-modern contrast was also of interest to the Russians: Grech's statements on the subject and Bestuzhev's title to his first "Glance" are only two of many treatments of the problem at this time. As in Europe, the contrast was related to the question of the "new" or "modern" school, as opposed to the "old" school of the Neoclassicists.

The most controversial aspect of Bestuzhev's "Glances" turned out to be his attempt to define the modern school in Russia. In his first "Glance" he stated that "with Zhukovsky and Batyushkov begins the modern school in our poetry," and he asserted further that "Alexander Pushkin, together with the two above-mentioned, makes up the triumvirate of our poetry." Elaborating on this attempt to unite the two leading Karamzinians with the younger poet who had already begun to dominate the generation of the 1820's, Bestuzhev pointed out that both Zhukovsky and Batyushkov "divined the secret of the majestic, harmonious Russian language. . . ." Zhukovsky is marked out for his "dreamy poetry" (which is to say "German" poetry), for his imagination, which enabled him to attain "the secret ideal of the beautiful," and for the idea that "many of [his] translations are superior to their originals." Batyushkov is characterized as having helped establish the modern school with his "languid sensualness and the passionate raptures of love," and he is praised as the Russian master of light verse, "the peer of Anacreon and Parny." What had been begun by these poets was capped by Pushkin: "While still a youth he amazed one and all with the forthrightness of his style, and in his first manhood he was given the secret of the Russian language, and the sorcery of poetry was revealed to him. A modern Prometheus, he stole the heavenly fire, and having made it his own, he plays capriciously with our hearts."[24]

In retrospect, Bestuzhev's assertions do not seem sensational, but at the time they were provocative. Praise for Zhukovsky meant praise for all that was signified by German Romantic poetry; Batyushkov's penchant for erotic verse had already become acceptable practice, but there were those who deplored it; and at just this time, 1823, Pushkin's Romantic verse tales were making his name synonymous with Romanticism in Russia. Above all, no one had yet dared to come out so strongly in favor of the modern school, to join these particularly controversial poets into a triumvirate, or to unite the two first generations of Romantics without mincing words. Nor did Bestuzhev's challenge go unanswered. "Just what does the author mean by *modern school*?" queried the editor of *Russian Invalid*, V. I. Kozlov. "If Romanism [*romanizm*, a word which was initially confused with *romantizm,* the Russian word for Romanticism], does he not know that this latter has at least as many opponents as defenders among our men of letters?" And, "did Zhukovsky and Batyushkov think of themselves as founders of a *modern school?* Did they proceed together along an identical path? . . ."[25]

Bestuzhev was not yet prepared to defend his opinion, however, and he parried by asking questions of his own. "All these questions are not to the point," he complained in *Son of the Fatherland.* "Why is the remark about opponents of the Romantic school brought up here? And why does Mr. Kozlov imagine that I contend Zhukovsky and Batyushkov to be its founders?" And taking advantage of Kozlov's improper use of terms, he asked: "Does he not assume that Romanticism and Romanism are one and the same thing? Of course Zhukovsky belongs to the modern school, but more as a translator than as an author; and as for Batyushkov, he has written only three works in the Romantic species. . . . Nevertheless it is obvious that while neither Zhukovsky nor Batyushkov thought of themselves as founders of a school . . . that is precisely what they are."[26] As will be shown, Bestuzhev's definition of the Russian modern school became a key assertion of his 1833 essay.

All of the ideas that Bestuzhev developed in his "Glances" were part of an attempt to express the literary position of *The Polar Star:* first, the Civic-Decembrist ideals of the almanac's two editors, and then the larger concerns of the Russian Romantic movement as a whole.[27] As has been stated, much of the almanac's influence was due to the timing of its appearance. In these years — 1823 to 1825 — the Romantics began to champion their cause openly, and the Romantic movement began to shift into more clearly defined literary positions and trends. Until the appearance in 1825 of *Northern Flowers,* the literary almanac of the Pushkin Pleiad, *The Polar Star* was the most powerful almanac in Russia.[28] Bestuzhev therefore occupied a most opportune position as regards the Romantic cause, and this obliged him to not only define the modern school, but to establish its legitimacy by emphasizing its continuity with the literary past. For this reason, his defense of the modern school is closely related to the main purpose of his first "Glance," as indicated by its title, "A Glance at Ancient and Modern Literature in Russia." His demonstration of continuity is embodied first, in the already discussed general comments on Russian conditions and second, in a systematic "catalogue" of critical evaluations of works and authors. This method of evaluation was a powerful and frequently used weapon of those critics who wished to establish standards of literary taste, and Bestuzhev used it with great effect.

Bestuzhev began his catalogue in the first "Glance" with comments on such important early Russian works as *The Song of Igor's Campaign*, the various chronicles, and the fifteenth-century military epic *Zadonshchina*. A broad jump is then made into the early eighteenth century, and it is here that Bestuzhev began to make his case for continuity. The essay contains succinct evaluations of Feofan Prokopovich and Antiokh Kantemir as prominent figures of the very early part of the century, and special attention is devoted to the contributions of Lomonosov. The latter is valued more highly than his contemporary Vasily Trediakovsky, who is treated rather coolly — and typically — as a literary pedant. The Neoclassical dramatist Alexander P. Sumarokov is hailed as "the father of our theater," and other mid-century figures such as Petrov, Kheraskov, Bogdanovich, Khemnitser, Fonvizin (lauded for his comedies), Kapnist, and Knyazhnin are mentioned. In all of these evaluations Bestuzhev was careful not to grant praise that could be interpreted as approval of Neoclassicism, and here he attacks Russian dependence on French culture.

When he arrived at the late eighteenth century, he began to make explicit claims for Romanticism, by lavishing praise on the best poet of the century, Derzhavin, characterizing him as the "foundation stone" of Russian Romanticism. His assessment is a repeat of a controversial phrase coined by Vyazemsky, who wrote an essay on the occasion of Derzhavin's death in 1817, proclaiming Derzhavin as the predecessor of the Romantics.[29] Bestuzhev did not call Derzhavin a Romantic, and he was equally careful not to name Karamzin a Romantic. Instead, Karamzin is seen as the "formulator" of modern literature because he "transformed the Russian language of books, sonorant, rich, and powerful in its essence. . . ." In Bestuzhev's opinion, Karamzin was important for his writing of Russia's first major history, *The History of the Russian State*, but he should be valued more highly for his "charming, colorful style [which] made a decisive turn for the better in our language."[30] The characterization is significant, because it not only relates Karamzin to the modern school on the basis of his language reforms, but it marks Bestuzhev's chief point of departure from the Karamzinian tradition. Decembrist Bestuzhev had no liking for Karamzin's pro-autocracy interpretation of Russian history, thus he was anxious to downplay the history by upgrading the style. This opinion is repeated in the later "Glances."

Bestuzhev treated a whole series of late eighteenth- and early nineteenth-century figures, including Maykov, Vostokov, the fabulist Izmaylov, and the dramatist Ozerov. Then, turning to the year 1822, he praised another list of writers: the fabulist Krylov, the great triumvirate of Zhukovsky, Batyushkov, and Pushkin, Baron Delvig, Davydov (valued for his "Amazon muse," a characterization of the hussar poet's verse of battle and bottle), Pletnyov, Kozlov, Bulgarin, Griboedov, and even Katenin (who is given deadpan mention as "the composer of ballads, criticism and anticriticism, and lyric verse").

Despite the great differences between all the poets Bestuzhev praised, there is one obvious trait they shared. They were all, in his opinion, "modern" poets whom he could treat equally within the purvey of that broad phenomenon known as "the new, the modern, the so-called Romantic school." Clearly he implied that they were the inheritors of the traditions established in the eighteenth century. This assumption is equally implicit in the second and third "Glances."

In the second, he gave strong preference to those poets who shared his commitment to the modern school. While he lamented the lack of originality in the literature of 1823, he concluded that Russian literature had advanced sufficiently to attract attention in Europe.[31] In the third "Glance" he again offered evaluations of such members of the modern school as Zhukovsky, Batyushkov, Kozlov, Yazykov, Odoevsky, Somov, Grech, and Bulgarin. He particularly praised Pushkin and thanked him for endowing Russian literature with two more Romantic verse tales, *The Fountain at Bakhchisaray* and *The Gypsies*, and the first chapter of *Eugene Onegin*.[32]

III *Bestuzhev the Translator*

The feud with Katenin did not, of course, comprise all of Bestuzhev's early contributions to the development of Russian literary criticism. Between 1819 and 1822 he published more than thirty articles, analyses, book reviews, feuilletons, and translations. He debated on a variety of literary subjects with such diverse men as Mikhail P. Bestuzhev-Ryumin, Vasily Perevoshchikov, N. V. Sushkov, Orest Somov, Pyotr Vyazemsky, Wilhelm K. Küchelbecker, and others. In 1821 he debated with Somov over Zhukovsky's translation of Schiller's ballad *Der Fischer*, and in the same year he battled with none other than Shishkov himself over the Shishkov-Karamzin positions. In 1820 he joined *The Free Society of*

Lovers of Literatures, Sciences, and the Arts headed by Izmaylov. Beginning in 1820 he contributed regularly to the journal *The Well-Intentioned*, and in 1821 he went over to the journal *The Champion of Enlightenment and Philanthropy*. Through most of the years until 1825 he contributed to Grech's *Son of the Fatherland*, and he was, of course, a regular contributor to his own almanac *The Polar Star* from 1823 through 1825. Undoubtedly, one of his most significant activities in this six-year period is represented by his translations.

It is apparent that as a translator Bestuzhev considered himself a conduit of Western literary ideas. Some twenty translations appeared in the years from 1820 to 1825 under the signature "A. Bestuzhev" or the familiar initials "A. B." There is a definite pattern to the order of appearance and subject of his translations. He translated from German, French, and English, but English criticism was his favorite occupation and he was especially attracted to essays in *The Edinburgh Review*. The translations are usually short revised versions of their originals, and they almost invariably deal with literature, although a few are political in nature.

In 1820 a translation entitled "On Taste" appeared in *The Well-Intentioned*, and this was quickly followed by a series of translations in *The Champion of Enlightenment and Philanthropy* under the titles "On Milton's *Paradise Lost* (From Blair)," "Thoughts of Various Authors, and Anecdotes," and "On the Romantic Character (From *Gossip's History*)" — all in 1820 and 1821. In 1822, "The Chief Periods of Danish Literature (From the Copenhagen Journal *Skilderie*)" appeared in *Son of the Fatherland* and "On the Tombs in the Thebes Catacombs" was published in *The Champion of Enlightenment and Philanthropy*. In 1824 various issues of the latter journal carried, in quick succession and sometimes two or three at once, "The Characters of Mary Stuart and Elizabeth: From Robertson," "The Passions Quarrel (From Miss Edgeworth)," "A Portrait Gallery, From English," "Learning, From Bacon," "Lord Chatham's Speech on the Question of the American Affair in 1777," and "The Pope's Letter to the Archbishop of Rochester." In the same year "Consolation in Misfortune (From Weiss)" was printed in Faddey Bulgarin's *Literary Leaves*, and in 1825 a long translation from French was published in *Son of the Fatherland* under the title "On the Spirit of Poetry of the XIX Century (Artaud)."

The most important of Bestuzhev's translations were undoubtedly "Esthetics: Oratory, From English" and "A Definition of Poetry: From English," which appeared in *The Champion of Enlightenment and Philanthropy* in 1824. Both are excerpts from

Wordsworth's influential "Preface to the 1801 Edition of *Lyrical Ballads*," and the latter begins with that famous definition: "All good poetry is the spontaneous overflow of powerful feelings and takes its origins from emotion recollected in tranquility." This is the first time the definition became generally known to Russians. Both Pushkin and Küchelbecker were greatly interested in it.

A curious item is *"Kenilworth*, A Novel by Walter Scott, A Critical Article from *The Edinburgh Review*," printed in 1824 in *The Champion of Enlightenment and Philanthropy*. Critical reviews of many of Scott's historical novels were published regularly in *The Edinburgh Review* at this time, but no review appeared on the novel *Kenilworth* or under this title. It was a not infrequent practice in Russia at this time to publish original works under the guise of translations, and, as will be shown, Bestuzhev did so at least twice. The translation — or original essay — is an analysis of *Kenilworth* and the methods and devices Scott used in the creation of authentic historical coloring. As must be shown in the context of Bestuzhev's historical prose tales, this aspect of Scott's creativity had a great influence on Bestuzhev, and it is possible that he was, indeed, the author of this item.

Although Bestuzhev the translator freely excerpted and edited his translations, he remained faithful to the originals. While "Thoughts of Various Authors, and Anecdotes" is an edited compilation, and the two translations from Wordsworth are excerpts, the translation of Blair's work on Milton's *Paradise Lost* is precise, and the translation of Wordsworth's definition corresponds exactly to the original. For a man considered to be a dedicated revolutionary at just this time, Bestuzhev was remarkably indifferent to sociopolitical materials. Only the translation of William Pitt's speech on the American Revolution may be construed as being of political interest. Most of the translations are related to Bestuzhev's concern for Romanticism. In light of his pride in his command of Polish, it is curious that no translations from this language have been traced to him. If the translation of the article on Danish literature is from Danish, it is an anomaly, for there is no evidence that Bestuzhev was able to read that language. It is likely that many of the anonymous translations of the 1820's and 1830's could be traced to Bestuzhev.

IV *Marlinsky the Theorist and the 1833 Essay*

The public career of Bestuzhev the critic ended with the Decembrist revolt. Not until the 1833 essay, "O romane N. A. Polevogo *Klyatva pri grobe Gospodnem*" ("On N. Polevoy's Novel *The Oath on the Tomb of the Lord"*) did Marlinsky the theorist make his appearance. This essay is significant for its literary criticism, but its evaluations are largely a repeat of the "Glances," and it is so much more important as Romantic theory that one scholar has even called it "a virtual manifesto of Russian Romanticism."[33] As a work in literary theory, it sums up the controversies that raged through the 1820's. As a work on the theory of history, it anticipates many of the philosophical questions that later divided the Russian intellectual world into Slavophiles and Westernizers. Ironically, it appeared too late to have an effect on the battle over Romanticism and too early to influence the later schism. This is to be regretted, because it is a link between the earlier and later struggles with the problem of Russia and the West. Curiously enough, although the essay's indebtedness to European Romantic philosophers has been mentioned by scholars, no one has attempted to trace its ideas to their specific sources; perhaps this is why its significance as a link has been overlooked. By 1833 Bestuzhev was thoroughly versed in Romantic Idealism, consequently, his essay is an attempt to synthesize some chief concepts of this body of thought into a Romantic-historical view of the history of world literature as a whole and of Russian literature in particular. When the sources of his ideas are properly traced and fully appreciated, it becomes possible to credit his essay as a major document in Russian intellectual history.

As has been noted, Romantic theory provided appropriate formulae in the 1820's for developing an original national literature while remaining responsive to Western influences. These formulae were adapted to the Russian historical experience as an integral part of the concept of *narodnost'*. The Romantics of the 1820's did not solve the problem of Russia and the West — it has not been solved yet — but they did manage to articulate many of its implications. The problem was implicit in Bestuzhev's debates of the 1820's, and he began his 1833 essay with a new statement of *narodnost'* that is remarkable for its use of prime concepts of Romantic Idealism.

"We live in an age of Romanticism," Bestuzhev declared. "That is the first thing. We live also in an age of history, moreover, in an age of history par excellence. History has always been with us, has always been inevitable. But at first it walked silently as a cat, crept stealthily as a thief. . . . Now history is not simply in fact, but in the memory, the mind, the heart of the people."

To Bestuzhev, as to the Romantic Idealist philosophers, the problem of history was the problem of a contrast between opposites, therefore he posed a dual division of history. "Here," he asserted, "is the dual — the Romantic-historic — trend of modern literature. It is necessary to state once and for all that by the term Romantic I mean the eternal striving of the infinite human spirit to express itself in finite forms. . . . And this is why I think that in spirit and essence there are only two literatures — there are the literatures before and since Christianity."

The key to history is not the customary split between Neoclassicism and Romanticism, or even between Classicism and Romanticism, but between ancient and modern modes of creativity, between pagan and Christian attitudes: "I would call the first a literature of *fate*, the second a literature of *will*. In the first dominate feelings and corporeal images; in the second reigns the soul, and ideas are dominant. The first is a place of execution where fate is the executioner, man the sacrifice; the second is a field of battle on which the passions fight with the will, over which from time to time there flashes the shadow of the hand of Providence."[34]

Bestuzhev's statement is important for its sophisticated use of the principle of contrast and its synthesis of several ideas conceived by Romantic Idealist philosophers. It is a direct restatement of an assertion by Madame de Staël in her well-known *De l'Allemagne* (1813; 1814), and thus an indirect adaptation of the ideas of her teacher August Schlegel and his brother Friedrich. In Madame de Staël's words: "We sometimes consider the word Classic as synonymous with perfection. I use it at present in a different acceptation, considering Classical poetry as that of the ancients, and Romantic as that which is generally connected with the traditions of chivalry. This division is equally suitable to the two eras of the world — that which preceded, and that which followed the establishment of Christianity." In her view the ancients "were completely the children of nature, and believed themselves controlled by fate, as absolutely as nature herself is controlled by necessity." Therefore, "the ancients, so to speak, possessed a corporeal soul and its emotions were all strong, decided, and consistent." And in other words quite similar to Bestuzhev's, she added: "In one it is fate which reigns, in the other it is Providence. Fate counts the sentiments of men as nothing; but Providence judges the actions according to these sentiments."[35]

Madame de Staël's *De l'Allemagne*, well-known to the Russians in the 1820's, served as a chief source of knowledge of the concept of national originality. Elaborating on her Christian-pagan interpretation of the ancient and modern periods, she wrote: "But our present object is not so much to decide between Classical and Romantic poetry, properly so called, as between the imitation of the one and the inspiration of the other. The literature of the ancients is, among the moderns, a transplanted literature; that of chivalry and romance is indigenous, and flourishes under the influence of our religion and institutions." In short, true creativity and originality have their only legitimate roots in the nation: ". . . the poetry written in imitation of the ancients, however perfect in its kind, is seldom popular, because, in our days, it has no connection whatever with our national feelings."[36]

As Bestuzhev realized, Madame de Staël's statements were indebted in their turn to some important assumptions of Romantic Idealist thought. According to these assumptions, the ancients had lived in a self-enclosed and finite world in which all phenomena were explainable in terms of fate. Their art was therefore unified, harmonious, and, above all, corporeal: it appealed directly to the physical senses. The moderns, on the other hand, had been accustomed to reflection and the infinite world of the imagination by Christian teachings, and they had inherited the medieval traditions of chivalry, love, romance, and mystery. Unlike the ancients, they were not at one with nature, and natural phenomena were not easily explainable. Modern art was therefore ideal (as opposed to real and corporeal): it gives rise to pictures in the mind — ideas — by appealing to the imagination rather than the senses. These assumptions were clearly articulated by the Schlegel brothers.

According to Friedrich Schlegel, the term Romanticism applied not only to the modern school, but to the entire tradition of Christian thought. He used the terms modern and Romantic first in his *Gespräch über die Poesie* (1800), seeing them as similar, but not identical: "Thus, I seek and find the Romantic with the older moderns, with Shakespeare, Cervantes, in Italian poetry, in that age of chivalry, love and fairy tales whence the thing and the word itself [Romance] are derived."[37] Therefore, the modern school was not something new, but rather, as Madame de Staël confirmed, a continuation of the traditions of chivalry. By implication, the Neoclassicists, with their misguided faith that the Greeks and Romans had discovered everything worth knowing about art and their belief that creativity should be based on imitation of the ancients, were a false anomaly in literary history. The true source of creativity is imagination and inspiration. Thus, because the ancients had also believed in inspiration, the Romantics, and not the Neoclassicists, were the true inheritors of antiquity. In his *Geschichte der alten und neuen Literatur* (1815), Friedrich Schlegel used all his authority as a scholar of antiquity to make this latter claim clear: "The Romantic is not opposed to the ancients, but to those false and frigid erudite among ourselves, who strain to imitate the form without being gifted with any portion of the enthusiasm of the antique. . . . The legends of Troy, and the poems of Homer, are throughout Romantic."[38]

August Schlegel was even more determined to establish the legitimacy of these assumptions about the Neoclassical-Romantic contrast. In his famous *Vorlesungen über dramatische Kunst und Literatur,* (published 1809 - 11), he made a harsh attack on the "fruitless" Neoclassical principle of imitation and then put forth the notion of contrast, declaring: "Perhaps in this idea we have discovered the true key to the ancient and modern history of poetry and the fine arts. Those who adopted it, gave to the peculiar spirit of *modern* art, as contrasted with the *antique* or *Classical*, the name *Romantic*. The term is certainly not inappropriate: the word is derived from *Romance.* . . ." Ancient art is corporeal, modern art is ideal, and therefore "the spirit of ancient art and poetry is *plastic,* but that of the moderns *picturesque.*" And in words which served as the basis of Madame de Staël's notions of fate and Providence, he concluded: ". . . the whole of the art and poetry [of the ancients] is the expression of a consciousness of the harmony of all their faculties. They invented the poetry of joy. . . . The very reverse of this is the case with the Christian view — everything finite and mortal is lost in the contemplation of infinity. . . . Hence, the poetry of the ancients was the poetry of enjoyment, and ours is that of desire — the former has its foundation in the scene which is present, while the latter hovers betwixt recollection and hope."[39]

Spirit, infinite, finite, fate, will, Providence, corporeal — Bestuzhev's opening statement is an erudite synthesis of statements which are the crux of the Romantic Idealist contrasts between ancient and modern, Classical and Romantic, pagan and Christian, alien and indigenous, the falsely imitative and truly creative. Having asserted this division of history, he then proceeded to outline the history of ancient and modern literatures. In his view, the ancient period was marked by three stages represented by three genres: the hymn of fear transformed into the hymn of triumph after man conquered nature; the épopée, "that is, the popular legends of the past

dressed in the finery of the fable" and conveyed to Greece from In-
dia via Persia; and the ancient drama, the tragedy to justify the
rulers and the comedy "which belonged solely to the people." Both
the épopée and the drama were created in Greece and conveyed to
Rome.[40] The outline is again Schlegelian — a compact restatement
of the treatment of antiquity in Friedrich Schlegel's *Geschichte*,
which also traces the history of world literature from its origins in In-
dia to Persia to Greece to Rome, from the hymn to the épopée to the
ancient drama.[41] Even more important is the fact that Bestuzhev's
adherence to Schlegelian thought is coupled with a denial of a
theory by a man who is considered the greatest influence on him —
Victor Hugo. "I don't remember who it was that first said that the
first poetry of all peoples is the hymn," Bestuzhev remarked. "At
least this opinion was given true coin by Victor Hugo. The opinion,
it is true, is brilliant, but it is not founded on anything of substance."
Contrary to Hugo's assertion, Bestuzhev believed that the first
human song was a cry of fear, a curse, or an incantation against evil.
Only later was the hymn born.[42] In his "Préface" to the drama
Cromwell (1827), Hugo suggested that the history of world literature
should be divided not into two, but three periods: primitivity (pre-
Homer), antiquity (from Homer to Christ), and a modern period
(from Christ to modern times). The primitive period was represented
by the hymn, the ancient period by the épopée and the ancient
drama, the modern period by the modern or, to use August
Schlegel's famous term, the Romantic drama.[43]

Bestuzhev also sided with the Schlegels against Hugo in his
characterization of the modern period. To the Schlegels, the term
Romantic was derived not only from *Romance*, but from *Roman*, the
word for the novel in the sense of both prose and verse narratives.
The dominance of the novel is central to Schlegelian thought,
despite August Schlegel's commitment to the drama in his major
work. In agreement with this, Bestuzhev characterized the modern
period as the history of the novel (the fourth generic stage): "After
the drama arises the novel, and it goes hand in hand with the
drama." The novel did not appear immediately, of course, for the
ancient world "fell fighting, fell after a long battle, and its arrows
remained deep in the body of the new warrior." The novel took centuries to develop, and this is why "the lamp of history is necessary for
us to discern in the gloom of the Middle Ages the path through the
ruins along which Romanticism invaded Europe from all sides and
finally took possession of her."[44] In Bestuzhev's view, the develop-

ment of Romanticism in the modern period was an "amalgamation" of the values of the East and the values of the North — "for the East is imagination and the North is intellect." Prior to this amalgamation, however, medieval Europe was characterized by what Bestuzhev called "practical Romanticism, Romanticism in action." With all its color and barbarism, the medieval period was most poetic: "Life did not just flow in that era of piety and love, that era of chivalry and brigandage. Hunters' horns trumpeted through the woods without cease, in the distance the abbey murmured with the peal of evening bells, the swords of knights-errant rang forth." The most important figures of this Gothic or Feudal era — Bestuzhev did not distinguish between the artistic and sociopolitical terms — were the wandering minstrels who "sang of glory and love, for at that time everyone loved glory and glorified love."[45]

Bestuzhev's amalgamation involves three martial events — the invasions of the Normans from the North, the Moors from the East, and the Crusades into the East and back. Although the Normans quickly forgot their Odin and their Valhalla, the spirit of their sagas, "the very spirit of the North," united with "the sharp-wittedness and vivacity of the Franks," and this spirit later penetrated into England, Spain, and Sicily. The invasions of the Moors brought "all the elegance of [the Arabic peoples'] poetry, their architecture, and their horsemanship," as well as designs, inlays, perfumes, and the art of serenading beneath balconies. "Soon their kaleidoscopic diversity of colors was reflected in all the poetry of the South and the West," and Bestuzhev found it important that "the Moor expressed himself in the speech of colors, similies, and hyperbole" and introduced rich rhymes and rhythms into European poetry. All of this dynamic process was crowned by the Crusades, as a result of which "literature grew rich with Eastern tales."[46]

Again Bestuzhev's thought is Schlegelian, and again his approach to ideas is synthetic — a reconciliation of opposites. Both Schlegel brothers believed that history advances by the force of martial activity, and a key tenet of their thought was that Western European civilization was born out of a synthesis of the Norman invasions and the Crusades. Bestuzhev does depart from the Schlegels, however, and this can be seen in his stress on the Moorish invasions. For this reason, his amalgamation is actually an attempt to synthesize the two opposing views of August Schlegel and Simonde de Sismondi that resulted in the great "North-South debate." The Schlegel brothers always insisted that Romanticism was a Northern, Norman,

Nordic, Germanic, Teutonic product, and this ethnocentrism was not appreciated by other Europeans.

In his *Geschichte,* Friedrich Schlegel asserted that "after the Crusades, perhaps, nothing had so much influence in giving a new direction to the imagination of the European nations as the expeditions of the Normans," and "the foundations of chivalry were indeed everywhere laid in the original modes of thinking of all the Germanic nations. . . ."[47]

August Schlegel was even more insistent on this point, and he went so far as to trace the key word Romance to "the name originally given to the languages which were formed from the mixture of Latin and the Old Teutonic dialects. . . ." Moreover: "After Christianity, the character of Europe has, since the commencement of the Middle Ages, been chiefly influenced by the Germanic race of Northern conquerors, who infused new life and vigor into a degenerated people. The stern nature of the North drives man back into himself; and what is lost in the free sportive development of the senses must, in noble dispositions, be compensated by earnestness of mind."[48] Just how carefully Bestuzhev read August Schlegel's *Vorlesungen* is indicated by his direct use of these words: "From the amalgamation of the carefree, frivolous, thoughtless, always singing Frenchman with the inhabitant of the stern North, who, having been shut all winter in his hut, and who was reluctantly forced back into himself and steeped in his own soul, came the inimitable humor which distinguishes our own age."[49]

Sismondi admitted the influence of the Normans, but he emphasized the influence on the Romance, rather than the Teutonic peoples. The purpose of his study of the literature of the South of Europe was to prove the influence of the Moorish invasions on the development of modern European civilization. The Germans, he maintained, had contributed little to that important age of chivalry: "We in vain attempt to discover, in the manners or traditions of the Germans, the birth of chivalry. . . . Gallantry was unknown to them, and their brave, loyal, but rude manners could never have contributed to the development of the sentiment and heroism of chivalry."[50] Given the prominence of the North-South debate, Bestuzhev was rather cavalier in the ease with which he handled the two contradictory viewpoints. Many of the Russians of the 1820's were aware of, and reacted to, the debate, but none of them, not even Pushkin,[51] dared to approach it so boldly. As will be shown, Bestuzhev's synthesis is crucial to his attempted solution of the problem of Russia and the West.

According to Bestuzhev, the age of chivalry was followed by the age of the bourgeoisie and then by the age of Neoclassicism in France. He treats both ages in great detail but makes no mention of the Renaissance. In his treatment of Neoclassicism he indicates great appreciation for Voltaire, Racine, and Moliére, but he makes his disapproval of the age clear.[52] This is nowhere more apparent than at the point where he turns his attention from Europe to Russia and makes the same point he had made in his earlier "Glances": that Russia had opened itself to the West at just the time French Neoclassicism reigned supreme, and had thus become vulnerable to the imitation of unnatural alien influences. "We became accustomed to living in the cast-off clothing and on the leavings of Paris," Bestuzhev complained, "without sorting the old from the new, the good from the bad." It was a time of such misplaced hope and slavish imitation that "as a Russian I blush at recalling it." Fortunately, however, even the Neoclassical age offered a ray of hope for "Romanticism had a representative even in this time of corporeality — this was the unfettered eccentric Rousseau." And the same was true for Russia, which had its Rousseau in the great Derzhavin: "A philosopher-poet, it was he who first laid the foundation stone of Russian Romanticism, not only in spirit, but also in the boldness of his images, the newness of his forms." Best of all, once Romanticism gained a foothold, it prospered, "and at last there shone forth the formulator of our modern poetry, Karamzin." Bestuzhev then proceeded to characterize eighteenth- and early nineteenth-century Russia exactly as he had evaluated it in the earlier "Glances."[53]

In turning to the Russian historical experience Bestuzhev once again brought himself face to face with the problem of Russia and the West, and he was presented with two tasks. First, having denounced Neoclassicism as alien, he was now hard put to assert a national originality for Romanticism. And second, he quickly showed himself anxious to draw a parallel between the European pattern of historical development and the Russian. He took on both tasks in their turn and if his attempt at a solution must be faulted as overly fanciful, it cannot be criticized for lack of ingenuity. He simply announced that Romanticism had conquered Russia as it had conquered Europe, thus implying that the two cultural experiences had been similar. "Romanticism triumphed, Idealism triumphed — and so what is all the fuss about?" he asked. "But we will not be vain. . . . We did not accept Romanticism, for it took us in battle, conquered us like the Tatars, so that no one perceived whence it came." And so Russia, almost ruined by Neoclassicism, was saved by Romanticism.

From Germany, "fallen into somnolence," came the melancholy dreaminess of Uhland, Goethe, and Schiller; from England, long since invigorated by Shakespeare, came the "spleen" of Byron. And here Bestuzhev once again took up his defense of the modern school. With the advent of the German-oriented Zhukovsky, the Italian- (i.e., South-) oriented Batyushkov, and the Byron-influenced Pushkin, Romanticism reached its full maturity in Russia. And besides, Bestuzhev asserted, taking up his second task, was Russia really so different from Europe? "With the exception of the Crusades and the Reformation, what did we not experience that Europe did?" he inquired. "A double-headed Janus, ancient *Rus* gazed simultaneously on Asia and Europe; her mode of existence comprised a link between the settled activity of the West and the nomadic indolence of the East. That is why there is such a diversity of relationships!"[54] In short, just as European civilization had been formed out of an amalgamation of the East (the Moors) and the North (the Normans), so Russia had been formed by the invasions of the Varangians (Normans) and the Tatars.

There is a disarming lack of equivocation in Bestuzhev's treatment of the process of history. He freely shuffled chronology and ignored whole eras of European history. Many of his statements are plainly erroneous, and many of his correct judgments are flawed by his penchant for hyperbole. This is nowhere more true than at the point where his enthusiasm prompts him to a faulty esthetic conclusion — his proclamation of the Romantic historical novel as the culmination of the entire Romantic process of history. Sir Walter Scott in Bestuzhev's opinion was the epitome of modern Romanticism, since he "determined the propensity of our age to historical details and created the historical novel which has now become a necessity from the walls of Moscow to Washington, from the magnate's study to the petty tradesman's counter." Of course, "Walter Scott is not a Romantic by theme, but he is a Romantic in exposition. . . . His very point of view toward the past shows that he is a poet — and that is enough. A poet in our age *cannot be other than* a Romantic!"[55] The judgment is wrong — neither Scott nor the historical novel proved to be the epitome of history — but it is perfectly correct in terms of the logic of Bestuzhev's essay. He had clearly reached a Schlegelian definition of Romanticism on the basis of its etymological relationship to the word *Roman* (the essay was even subtitled "On

Romanticism and the Novel"), and thus the historical novel had to be the ultimate synthesis of that "dual direction" of world history, both Romantic and historical. This is what he meant when he asserted that "we live in an age of Romanticism . . . we live also in an age of history," and this is the conclusion toward which he was moving throughout his colorful treatment of history.

This was not, however, his final conclusion. In his terms, as in terms of Romantic Idealism, history is a perpetual process, and the Romantic historical trend promised far more than the novels of Scott. "We live in an age of history," Bestuzhev had proclaimed, and he now set out to prove where the final reconciliation of Romanticism and history would lead. The discovery of the German *Nibelungenlied*, the Scandinavian *Edda*, the Carolingian manuscripts, and the Slavic *Song of Igor's Campaign* had revived a widespread interest in history. In Russia the twelve volumes of Karamzin's *History of the Russian State* and the three volumes which had already appeared of Nikolay Polevoy's *History of the Russian People* had given Russians a knowledge of their national past, a source for their historical themes, and a pride in their national originality. To the glory of Russian literature there had already begun to appear the historical novels of Bulgarin and Zagoskin, Masalsky and Lazhechnikov, Zotov and Kalashnikov, to say nothing of Pushkin's Romantic historical drama *Boris Godunov*, Nikolay Polevoy's historical novel *The Oath on the Tomb of the Lord*, and, above all, "the historical tales of Marlinsky, in which he cast off the fetters of the language of books and spoke forth in the living Russian vernacular." Consequently, there could be no doubt where the Romantic historical novel would reach its greatest glory. The history of Russia was richer and more full of adventure than the history of any other European nation, and Russian writers could not but be inspired by their national past. Russian Romanticism, in all the glory of its *narodnost'*, would push Russian literature to the forefront of world literary history, and the Russian Romantic historical novel would thereby become the final realization of the Romantic development of history.[56]

Looking back on the turbulent rise of Romanticism and the brilliance of the Pushkin period, it is not difficult to discover that Alexander Bestuzhev was one of the most active and influential men of letters. As a translator, critic, editor, polemicist, authority on language, literary and historical theorist, he was an activist who did much to determine the direction taken by Russian literature. His career was interrupted by the revolt of December 14, 1825, but the years in which he exerted his influence, 1819 - 25, were crucial years, and he was therefore able to play a prominent role in the reforms which paved the way for the development of a great national literature. If he was sometimes too visceral in his criticism and based his early reputation too strongly on sarcastic wit, his judgments were reinforced by detailed stylistic and linguistic analyses which established relevant standards of literary taste. One of the most erudite Russian students of European Romantic thought, he was especially talented in the application of literary theory to Russian conditions. His esthetic judgments were sometimes faulty, most noticeably in his evaluation of the historical novel, but it cannot be denied that he was often correct in his estimates of what would and would not endure in Russian literature: the *slavianshchina* as an unreliable linguistic position, the greatness of Zhukovsky as a translator, Derzhavin as the greatest poet of the eighteenth century, *narodnost'* as a problem of both language and history, Neoclassicism as an outworn set of literary rules, literature as the vehicle of historical progress, the great promise Russian literature would fulfill for the world. One of the best critics of his time, he did much to make literary criticism an esteemed profession in Russia.

CHAPTER 3

Alexander Bestuzhev: The Early Prose — 1820-25

W HEN Alexander Bestuzhev wrote his first prose tale in 1821, Russian literature had no significant tradition of prose fiction. Both the Neoclassical insistence on and the early Romantic preference for verse ensured that interest in prose remained desultory. Eighteenth-century Russians enjoyed translations, or rather, the frequently awkward improvisations of European prose works, which passed as translations, and a number of writers wrote stylistically awkward stories, tales, and novels which pretended at originality. The prose of literary criticism and journalism became well established in the eighteenth century, and the Russians adopted the Neoclassical tradition of elegant correspondence. In the 1790's prose enjoyed a modest vogue in the Sentimental epistolary works of Alexander Radishchev and Nikolay Karamzin, and the latter's Sentimental tales and stories achieved widespread popularity for a time. In the early nineteenth century Karamzin's Sentimental prose was widely imitated, and even Zhukovsky wrote one prose tale. But as late as the 1820's prose works were more apt to be unimaginative adaptations or loose translations rather than products of literary originality. Poetry remained supreme — this was after all the decade of Russia's great national poet. Russian literature underwent a transition from verse to prose only in the 1830's. It is little wonder, then, that Bestuzhev enjoyed far more success in the early 1820's as a critic than as a prose writer, since in his early career he was almost alone as a writer of prose tales.

I "Instigator" of the Russian Prose Tale

The lack of a significant prose tradition was therefore a key factor in Bestuzhev's chosen genre, the prose tale. He could and did develop his genre on the foundation laid by such predecessors as Karamzin, whose influence is important to understanding how

Bestuzhev began developing his genre. But the Russian prose tradition was so scant, and Bestuzhev found the Sentimentalist manner so unpromising for his needs as a Romantic writer, that he had to turn either to the European tradition for his models or devise his own methods. Belinsky realized this perfectly when he noted: "In the twenties were revealed the first attempts to create a true prose tale. This was the time of a universal reform which appeared as a consequence of the initial acquaintance with German, English, and the new French literatures, and of sensible concepts of the laws of creativity. . . . In order not to say too much, I will say that Mr. Marlinsky was our first teller of tales, he was the creator, or more properly speaking, the instigator *[zachinshchik]* of our Russian prose tale."[1]

The necessity to rely on European models and at the same time develop original techniques thus became two more factors in Bestuzhev's "instigation" of the Russian Romantic prose tale. A fourth factor, and perhaps the most important, is that just at this time the Romanticism of the Karamzinians was maturing into the fully Romantic endeavors of the men of the 1820's. Thus, Bestuzhev's works are not simply prose tales, but Romantic prose tales. In his literary opinions, in the nature of his prose tales, and in his personal character, Bestuzhev is a prime example of Russian Romantic creativity. To him, Romanticism was a supreme value, and Belinsky did not exaggerate one whit when he proclaimed: "The false idea of false Romanticism so overwhelmed our *romantic* critic that . . . everyone talented and gifted is a Romantic. Romanticism in Marlinsky's eyes is the alpha and omega of truth, the foundation stone of the world, the key to every bit of wisdom, the solution to all on the earth and under the earth, the solution to the most omnipotent enigmas, from the wart on an old crone's nose to the secret thoughts of a genius."[2]

The prose tale occupies a more definitive place in the inventory of Russian literature than it has enjoyed in American letters. In American criticism prose genres are usually defined in terms of length or number of words, with a scale drawn between the short story and the novel. References are made to long short stories and short novels, and the term novella is used to describe a prose work falling in the median area.[3] Russians, on the other hand, use distinct terms — short story *(rasskaz)*, prose tale *(povest')*, and novel *(roman)* — and they make reference not only to the length of a work, but its generic character. Thus, the short story is usually discussed in terms not only of brevity, but of theme or content. The novel is defined not simply as "a long work," but also as one with "a complicated plot." The prose tale is defined quite differently from the other two genres, and it is not a novella in the American meaning of that term. Russian dictionaries define it as "an artistic work of a narrative character, smaller in dimension than the novel," and in fact the word *povest'* means "narrative." The word is sometimes used for a verse work, but in standard practice it signifies a prose tale. During the Romantic period the prose tale was first the rival and then the successor of the verse tale, and it has remained popular as a genre to this day.

As for the distinctive character of Bestuzhev's prose tale, several initial statements may be offered. To begin with, it is not a singular, uniform genre which may be easily defined, but rather a broad and variegated literary form that answers to a surprisingly large number of thematic demands. At times his tales are so short as to tempt the label short story, and a few are so long as to get perilously close to the novel. But despite their range in length, despite even their variegation in plot, theme, structure, and subject, they always manage somehow to remain essentially the same in narrative type. They are unified further by the vigorous intrusion of the author's own personality, and especially by their unmistakably "Marlinistic" style.

There is a clearly discernible pattern to the development of the genre. Developed through the two periods that mark Bestuzhev's interrupted career, it falls into integrally related generic categories — that is, there is a close relationship between the forms of his tales and their themes. Themes and structures occur and recur and are blended into new forms which are developed from tale to tale, category to category, period to period, thus revealing the continuous development of a single prose writer. The genre stands as a series of related forms sharing distinctive features and cultivated within the confines of distinctive generic categories. These categories are five in number and they correspond chronologically to the two periods.

Bestuzhev's first period lasted from 1821 through 1825, when he was arrested for his part in the Decembrist revolt. This period is characterized by two generic categories — the tales of history and the early tales of men and passions. The second period lasted from 1830 to Bestuzhev's death in 1837. It is comprised of the later tales of men and passions, the sea stories, the tales of horror, and the tales and essays of the Caucasus.

II   *The Tales of Livonian History: Walter Scott*

By early 1821 Bestuzhev was established in Russian letters as a poet, critic, and translator. The publication at this time of an

epistolary prose work entitled *Poezdka v Revel'* ("Journey to Revel")
encouraged him to turn to fiction. The epistolary work, which is both
a travel journal and a historical account of the Baltic region in the
Middle Ages, served as the basis for the writing of a series of
historical tales known as the Livonian cycle. His decision to choose a
non-Russian subject for his first tales is both ironic and natural. On
the one hand, he shared the deep conviction of his contemporaries
that the creation of a national and Romantic literature must entail a
concentration on Russian themes, this conviction being a chief demand of the concept of *narodnost'*. At the same time, however,
Bestuzhev was aware of the importance of the age of chivalry to
Romantic esthetics, and his exposure to the architectural remnants of
the Middle Ages, especially the many Gothic castles, awakened an
avid interest in the historical past of the Baltic peoples. Added to this
motivation was still another value important to a man determined to
write Romantic tales: the historical past of the Germanic-Teutonic
peoples of the Baltic could not but seem exotic to Russian readers.
The Livonian cycle comprises *Journey to Revel* and several minor
pieces, with the core of the cycle formed by three Gothic or "castle"
tales — *Zamok Venden* ("Castle Wenden", 1821), *Zamok
Neygauzen* ("Castle Neihausen," or Neihusen, 1824), and *Zamok
Eyzen* ("Castle Eisen," 1825; first published as *Blood for Blood*);
and a Scottian tale entitled *Revelsky Turnir* ("Tournament at
Revel," 1825). The castle tales are the least complex and
sophisticated of the early tales, and they demonstrate the nature of
Bestuzhev's early talent most clearly.

The immaturity of the castle tales is a pronounced feature of their
literary quality, and this is revealed best by their ingenuous subjects
and plots. *Castle Wenden* tells the story of the first Magister of the
Order of Swordbearers *(Schwertbrüderorden)* Winno von Rohrbach,
who mistreats the vassals of Sir Wigbert von Serrat and then refuses
to duel with the knight of lower rank. In quest of honor and revenge,
Serrat creeps into Castle Wenden at night and brutally murders his
enemy.

Castle Neihausen treats the adventures of a fourteenth-century
Novgorodian warrior held prisoner in Livonia. It is a tale of
marvelous coincidences, told with swift action and heroic
pronouncements. Its hero rescues his own captor from villainous in-
triguers, learns that his captor's beautiful wife is his very own sister,
and successfully negotiates a Novgorod-Livonian peace pact.

Castle Eisen is the story of Baron Bruno von Eisen, a brutal giant who terrorizes his peasants. When Bruno is murdered by his young wife and nephew, his twin brother returns to Castle Eisen, poses as his brother's ghost, murders the young hero, and buries the heroine alive.

The castle tales, then, are disappointingly immature and conventional. They are also plagued by false heroics and affected dialogue. *Castle Wenden,* for example, is filled with such heroic pronouncements as "Desist, Rohrbach!" "For me there can be no jesting where the suffering of humanity is concerned!" and "Revenge and death to the Magister!" There are, however, some saving graces in the tales, and they are important as proof of the talents Bestuzhev later developed into his specialities. The first of these is the style, particularly the style of the descriptive passages. A few of these passages are quite good, showing that Bestuzhev was able, right from the start of his career, to recreate the color and poetry of the historical past. *Castle Wenden* is again a good example, for it is imbued with a faintly colored mist of medieval atmosphere. The tale, brief and simple, concentrates on only two short events — the offense and the revenge — yet the author manages to work several fine descriptions into his narrative, one being this tranquil description of Wenden at night:

At last the Pater raises his voice in the evening prayer, and the castle people kneel and read after him the *Credo* and the *Ave Maria.* Their bows to the ground bring the prayers to an end, each kisses the crucifix; and then lights glimmer along the corridors, voices whisper, reverberating softly back and forth, but soon even the rustle of footsteps falls silent and a deep torpor reigns throughout. The golden-rayed moon barely shines through the clouds; the drowsing woods stand without a stir and the black shadows of the castle towers lie motionless on the surface of the waters of the moat. From time to time a waft of winged breeze waves the skirts of the Meisterherr's banner, and then it subsides once more to enfold the staff. Only the measured ring of the sentry's broadsword resounds along the castle walls. Now leaning on his lance, he plunges his gaze into the dark distance, now lost in dreams of forsaken homeland, of faraway beloved, he croons a song from the ancient past. (I, 42)[4]

A second feature of the Livonian tales is quite unusual. In fact, it could very well be a literary talent without significant precedent or successor in all Romantic literature. Despite Bestuzhev's fanciful imaginative storytelling, his prose tales are striking for their careful authenticity. There seem to be no significant limits to his determination to found each tale on thorough research, since each tale is reinforced by precise historicity. Even a cursory reading of *Journey to Revel* shows that during his visit to the Baltic area, he exerted great effort to see and study the area's history, architecture, ethnography, economy, social and political institutions — in fact, every possible nuance and facet. The Soviet scholar Vasily G. Bazanov has examined Bestuzhev's research into the Baltic area, and he notes that preparation for the Baltic trip began as early as 1818 with Bestuzhev's first translation, a German study of serfdom in the area. He points out that Bestuzhev was familiar with Ernst Moritz Arndt's *Der Geist der Zeit,* and Bestuzhev refers to Arndt throughout his Livonian works. He acknowledges that his own brief history of Revel, in *Journey to Revel,* is a précis of Arndt's study. Bestuzhev was also familiar with the Sofian Chronicle *(Sofijsky vremennik),* and through Arndt he became familiar with the famed Livonian Chronicle, *Heinrich's Chronik.* Bazanov believes that a fragment of a history of the Latvians located in the Bestuzhev archives and annotated as a translation from German is actually an original study by Bestuzhev.[5] And finally, it has recently been proved that Bestuzhev is the author of a short history of Livonia published in 1829.[6]

Bestuzhev's concern for authenticity is further indicated in that each of his historical tales is based on an actual event. *Castle Wenden* treats the actual murder of the Magister by Serrat in 1208. *Castle Neihausen* is a dramatization of actual events leading to a Novgorod-Livonian alliance in the fourteenth century. The events and characters of *Castle Eisen* are real, incorporating Bestuzhev's research on the history of the castle after he visited the ruins. All the tales of Russian history are based on events treated in Karamzin's *History of the Russian State.* The tales also contain expository passages which treat a great many authentic matters. *Castle Neihausen* contains a dramatization of the *Femegerichte,* the dread secret trials which originated in Germany and spread to Livonia before they could be outlawed by the chivalric orders. *Tournament at Revel* is filled with discussions of medieval customs, and one whole chapter is devoted to an account of the bourgeois period that became important to the 1833 essay. Bestuzhev became an authority on Gothic architecture while in the Baltic, and his tales contain many discussions of the subject. So enthusiastic was he about his subjects that he inserted dozens of footnotes to his tales as a means of documenting various subjects and fictional treatments of customs and historical events.

Because Bestuzhev was so obviously intent on imparting authenticity to his prose tales, some scholars have had no difficulty finding evidence for interpretations of his literary manner as Realist or, at least, "tendency toward Realism."[7] Nevertheless, the careful authenticity of the tales, and their author's almost pedagogical zeal for communicating scholarly knowledge to his readers, are very much in keeping with Romantic esthetics. Bestuzhev's stress on authenticity does not reveal a similar concern for credibility in his literary manner. Rather, it represents his concern for *narodnost'*, in the sense of national color, and *mestnost'*, the Russian equivalent of the Romantic notion of local color. There is no indication in Bestuzhev's prose tales, not even in his last tales, that he practiced a careful selectivity of detail aimed at achieving credibility or convincing his readers that his stories are "real." To the contrary, his enthusiasm for authenticity and scholarly facts is part of his eager acceptance of the Romantic value of imagination, and it is apparent that he is interested in the color, excitement, fascination, even sensationalism of his subject matter. His concern for authenticity is part of his love of the exotic, the extreme, the unusual. His enthusiasm for facts conveys a sense of excitement and betrays a determination to stimulate the imagination with fascinating materials. And despite the care he devoted to accuracy of details, it is always evident that he strove to create or recreate the color, rather than the reality, of his subject, be that subject history, sea lore, or Caucasian exoticism.

Above all, Bestuzhev's concern for authenticity reflects his desire to transform the theory of *narodnost'* into a viable literary practice, demonstrated with particular clarity by the tales of the Livonian cycle. It will be remembered from the previous chapter that Bestuzhev first developed his interpretation of the concept of *narodnost'* as basically a problem of language. He also used language as his vehicle for conveying *narodnost'* in his literary manner, and, in so doing, he developed a most unusual literary technique. For Bestuzhev, the key to the reconstruction of the historical past and the creation of authentic atmosphere in a literary work was language, and he expressed this conviction many times, perhaps most lucidly in his Caucasian essay, *"Put' do goroda Kuby"* ("The Route to the Town of Kuba," 1836): "Language alone, independent of any merits historical or poetic, is the unlimited key to discovery; from its gait it is possible to discern the course of enlightenment and the capacity of ideas *(la portée des idées)* of every people." (II, 188)

Throughout his career Bestuzhev filled his tales with colorful atmosphere by using language so astonishing to his readers with its profusion of authentic terms that his technique can be appropriately called saturation. In his tales from Livonian and Russian history, in his sea stories, in his ethnographic sketches, and above all in his exotic tales of the Caucasus, he saturated entire passages with authentic words, terms, phrases, and foreign expressions. There is both a literary and a pedagogical intent to his use of the device, and he even provided his readers with a multitude of etymological observations and footnotes scattered through his works. More than any writer of his time, he used language to penetrate into a historical era, geographical area, or technical subject, and make it an entertaining literary feature.

The device of saturation is especially important to the Livonian tales, for Bestuzhev relied on it to convey the exoticism of the medieval period in the Baltic area. *Castle Wenden* owes a great deal of its sound and color of history to the extensive use of dated and localized terms. Weaponry is an important subject of the tale, which is filled with the Russian words for "sword," "dagger," "standard of arms," "knight's collar," "jerkin," "plates of iron gloves," and "half-boots." *Tournament at Revel* is also replete with terms of weaponry such as "visor," "lance," "cuirass," "shields," "faceplate," "horsecloth," "armor," "streamer," "helmet," "spurs," "stirrups," "platband," and "embroidered skirts and horsecloths." Significant historical coloring is accrued to the Livonian tales by the use of German names and, especially, titles. In *Castle Wenden* Bestuzhev employs the titles Magister and vassal, as well as the Russian equivalent for the German term Schwertbrüder. In *Castle Neihausen* he uses the titles Baroness, Herrmeister, Page, Rothmeister, Freigraf, and Grossmeister, usually in Cyrillic transcription. Terms of heraldry are of great importance to the Livonian tales, and *Tournament at Revel* is filled with such terms as Ratsherr, Baron, Herald, Bürgermeister, Landrath, Witzbetreber, as well as the Russian equivalents for Brother of the Order, and Seine Durchlaucht. Gothic architecture is another prominent subject of the tales, and this type of terminology lends even more local and historical color. *Castle Neihausen* opens with a description of a Gothic castle with "circular walls," "gates," "wide yard," "towerchambers," "turrets," "windows with marvelous decorations," "contraforces," "double-tiered crosswalks," "foundations," "abutments," "Gothic windows," "gabled vaults," "jagged walls," and "wall arquebus." As the narrator of the tale recalls his visit to the ruins of Castle Neihausen he remembers that "only one circular tower of Gothic architecture was still standing. . . ." Even *Tournament at Revel,* which is not a castle tale, mentions that the walls of a great hall were eaten by time and worms, the corners were festooned with spider webs, a stove with twelve legs stood in one corner, and on the wall to the right hung the family portraits and a huge pedigree.

The three castle tales adhere to the Romantic tradition of the Gothic Revival, and this can be seen in the themes of blood, revenge, and sweet terror. But as will be shown in discussion of the tales of horror, Bestuzhev was not fully aware of the nature or implications of the Gothic novel when he wrote the tales of the Livonian cycle. This is indicated most readily by his employing details not so much to create an atmosphere of mystery and terror (the use of Gothic accoutrement) as to revive the historical past. The castle tales are more properly historical, rather than Gothic, and it is apparent that Bestuzhev's first and most prominent interest was history. This gives immediate rise to the question of the influence of Sir Walter Scott. Bestuzhev valued Scott very highly, and in his discussion of the introduction of Romanticism into Russia, in the 1833 essay, he asserted: "Together with the appearance of the German somnolence and the English spleen, Holy Russia was graced by still another unexpected but welcome guest — I speak of the historical novel. The genius of Walter Scott divined the domestic life and daily thought of chivalric times. . . . Yes, Walter Scott sprinkled them with the living water of his creative imagination, breathed into them, and said — 'Live' — and they came to life with the bloom of life in their cheeks, with the pulse of realness in their breasts." (II, 593) Again, in his Caucasian essay "The Route to the Town of Kuba" Bestuzhev contended: "Up to the present time we have found the novel in history. Walter Scott contrived to dress history in the novel. I am amazed that the historical novel is called the illegitimate son of invention and truth! Does it perhaps have a different kinship, a different genealogy from its older sister? There is little truth in Walter Scott's historical figures, but is there any more in the portraits of Plutarch? I contend that the domestic man is more easily divined than the political!" (II, 187)

What Bestuzhev admired about Scott, therefore, was his ability to recreate authentic historical atmosphere in all its most intimate, its most everyday, its most "domestic" facets. In his Livonian tales he employed Scott's glorification of the past in all its pageantry, and it should not be overlooked that, like Scott, he preferred "to err on the side of colloquiality rather than on that of correctitude," that is, to value the color of history more than historicity.[8] The only significant way in which Bestuzhev differs from Scott in this matter is that he was far more language-oriented. Bestuzhev was also influenced by Scott in that he detected a key aspect of his historical novels — the device of dramatizing the dilemma of the hero caught on the threshold of a new epoch. The plot of a novel by Scott depends on its complicated situations, which stem almost always from the dilemma of the hero who is torn by a conflict of loyalty. He is committed and sympathetic to the old epoch, yet unable to deny the reality of the new. Here, however, there is a sharp difference in the attitudes of the two writers. Where Scott's sympathies usually lie with the old, Bestuzhev is always sympathetic to the new, and he takes a Civic-Decembrist satisfaction in affirming the victory of new over old.

The historical prose tale most deeply obligated to Scott is *Tournament at Revel*. "You are accustomed to seeing the knights of old through the tinted glass of their castles," Bestuzhev notes in his epigraph to the tale. "Now I will throw open the door of their abode for you, I will show them close at hand and in their full truth." Set in fourteenth-century Revel, the tale is about the lowly but young merchant Edwin and his love for Minna, the lovely daughter of Sir Bernhard von Burtneck. Unable to marry above his station, Edwin disguises himself as a knight and enters a tournament where he defeats a haughty rival and wins Minna's hand in marriage. Clearly intended to dramatize the contrast between the once vigorous, now foppish age of chivalry with the strong new age of the bourgeoisie, the tale affirms the virtues of bourgeois institutions. In Chapter I, for example, an Italian guest pokes fun at Burtneck's pride of ancestry and lack of personal accomplishment. In Chapter II the chivalry-bourgeois contrast is developed further by a revelation of Minna's contempt for the milksop suitors among the knights of Revel and by the development of Edwin's more manly and heroic character. The age of chivalry is subjected to ridicule in the person of a third rival, a comic character, and by Edwin's descriptions of the pompous noblemen assembled to watch the tournament. The vigor of the bourgeoisie is underscored again by a digressive chapter which treats the institution of Schwartzen-Häupter, the order through which am-bitious merchants could buy or win their way into the ranks of chivalry.

The tale treats what is usually the culmination point of the

Romantic historical novel or the traditional Romance of Chivalry and it is quite similar to the motif of the tournament of honor in Scott's *Ivanhoe*. It happens also to be based on the account of an actual event which Bestuzhev found in *Heinrich's Chronik*. Plagued by false heroics and affected character speech, it is relatively more complex in structure — as indicated by its skillful fusion of such elements as digression, exposition, espistolary interludes, and witty dialogue to advance the action and provide historical color. It is a tale filled with the color and pageantry of history, and its historicity is enhanced by Bestuzhev's knowledgeable use of terms for architecture, weaponry, clothing, and heraldry.

III   *The Tales of Russian History: N. M. Karamzin*

The Livonian cycle is organically related to the Russian cycle of historical tales. That is, despite obvious differences in setting and subject, the tales of the cycles are similar in form and style. The tales of Russian history are *Gedeon* (1821), *Roman i Ol'ga: Starinnaya Povest'* ("Roman and Olga: A Tale of Olden Times," 1823), *Izmennik* ("The Traitor," 1825), and *Naezdy: Povest' 1613 goda* ("The Raiders: A Tale of the Year 1613," 1831). The cycle is heavily influenced by Karamzin, and the themes were taken from Karamzin's *History of the Russian State*. Bestuzhev also consulted Karamzin's historical tales. *Roman and Olga* is indebted to Karamzin's *Natalya, the Boyar's Daughter* (1792) and to *Marfa Posadnitsa* (1803) for the description of the Novgorod *veche*, the ancient gathering of citizens to decide public affairs. The Gothic atmosphere of Karamzin's *Bornholm Island* (1793) had a decided influence on Bestuzhev's Livonian tales with their castle settings. The epistolary work *Journey to Revel* is modeled on Karamzin's *Letters of a Russian Traveller* (1791 - 1801). The affected speech of some of Bestuzhev's early prose tales is in keeping with Karamzin's literary manner.[9]

But if Bestuzhev leaned heavily on Karamzin and was in very many ways a continuator of the Karamzin reforms, the differences between the manners of the two men are most revealing. Those differences are the differences between Sentimentalism and Romanticism. The most salient feature is that Bestuzhev's tales are far more virile than Karamzin's. In sharp contrast to the charmingly sentimental style of Karamzin's most well-known tale, *Poor Liza* (1792), Bestuzhev's tales are vigorously masculine and boldly stated. The tamest of his heroes is always too busy fighting bloody battles to gather lilies from the fields of Karamzin's pastoral settings. Where

Karamzin's heroes indulge themselves in personal sentiment, without ever becoming strongly emotional, Bestuzhev's heroes of the early tales are bold, forthright, and brave. Their speech is seldom saccharine sweet, but rather, heroic. The only real exception to this rule is *Roman and Olga*, and even this sometimes coyly phrased tale is more vigorous than Karamzin's Sentimentalism.

There are also some relevant political differences between the two writers, and this sets the nature of their respective tales apart. Where Karamzin was studiously apolitical in his belles-lettres and pro-autocracy in his writing of history, Bestuzhev, the Decembrist, was overtly political in his early tales and firmly anti-autocracy in his guarded criticisms. *Roman and Olga*, written on the theme of Novgorod as the symbol of ancient Russian democracy, is a polemic with Karamzin; all of Bestuzhev's tales of history portray heroes who defend the common people from tyrants. Bestuzhev's political differences with Karamzin cannot be stressed too strongly, for they had a profound effect on his tales. Pointing exclusively to the political orientation of Bestuzhev's *Journey to Revel*, the Soviet scholar Bazanov has gone so far as to suggest that "it has nothing in common with Karamzin's 'literature of travel.' "[10]

Roman and Olga is probably the most representative of Bestuzhev's tales of Russian history, but the best tale is *The Traitor*. The tale is based on an account in Karamzin's *History of the Russian State* of Vladimir Sittsky, a prince of Pereyaslavl who in 1610, at the height of the second Polish intervention in Russia during the Time of Troubles, went over to the interventionist camp and was killed during the storming of his own city. In both theme and execution it is an excellent tale, and it shows that the early Bestuzhev was able to create a mood of dread and a feeling of suspense. The tale became a Russian favorite, and it is little wonder that an adolescent Turgenev wrote to his uncle in 1831: "Yesterday for the first time in my life I felt an indescribable agitation and an upheaval through my entire inner being, from reading Bestuzhev's *The Traitor*. I tried twice to read it to the end — and was unable!"[11]

The superiority of this tale is best demonstrated by its relative depth of theme and its unusual structure. Vladimir Sittsky is a man torn between his fanatic desire for power and his pitiful longing for the admiration of his fellow Russians. His torment is all the stronger for his hatred of his younger brother and his jealousy over the girl they both love. It is the psychology of his envy that effects the tale's tragedy. The work consists of five chapters, each of which is a blend of motif, situation, and setting. It progresses steadily from chapter to chapter, with an adept linkage of motifs into an organically developed main theme. The plot structure is similar to that of a five-act drama, and it is no accident that the tale is fitted with an epigraph from Shakespeare's *Othello* beginning: ". . . Never pray more; abandon all remorse." Unlike *Roman and Olga*, the chapters of *The Traitor* are not tedious little packages of adventure, for Bestuzhev combines and re-combines his structural elements across chapter boundaries.

A short first chapter begins with Vladimir's return to his peaceful Pereyaslavl homeland, and the reader's curiosity is aroused by allusions to his nebulous past. The second chapter is set in an unmistakably Shakespearian scene on the city's walls at night, where a sentry and a carpenter discuss Vladimir's unexpected return, the vague rumors about his past, and the contrast between his dark personality and his sincerely admired brother. The main situation — the conflict between two dissimilar brothers — is thus blended into two chapters with two settings and a single motif: the general distrust of the hero. Where Bestuzhev's careful handling of structural elements can be appreciated best is in the development of the theme of envy.

In Chapter Three, Vladimir performs a terrible act of witchcraft in a dark stormy woods. In the violent words with which he calls upon unclean powers for the fulfillment of his desire for power, he reveals the depth of his hatred, envy, and ambition. At the same time he betrays the lengths to which he will go to achieve his ends, even to the point of sacrificing his last human trait — his pitiful longing for admiration.

In Chapter Five, after suspense has been brought to a peak by Vladimir's decision to betray his homeland, the hero is himself allowed to bare his past, his character, and his motivations. In the swarming camp of the interventionists, he sits through the night with the mercenary leader Lisovsky and confesses his debauchery in Moscow during the reign of Boris Godunov and his crafty opportunism during the first intervention. He reveals his jealousy over his brother's fiancée and shows that he is prepared to sacrifice even his ambitions to revenge himself on the young lovers. He has shed the last of his humanity, and his motivations are now concentrated into one evil joy: "With whom and for what to fight has never been important to me — only to ruin and destroy. This pastime has become my goal, this goal my reward. My soul lights up in the dust of battle; I become more alive with each life I take from others." (I, 145 - 46)

It is thus inevitable that Vladimir will murder his brother during the bloody storming of Pereyaslavl and that he will himself die branded as a fratricide and traitor.

A significant feature of *The Traitor* is its unusual use of a Shakespearian play as a structural model. Its five chapters are either juxtaposed or blended, much like a five-act drama. The theme is historical, and its focus on the inner motivations of the hero helps to achieve much of that keen analysis of "The Quivering Heart of a Man" which the Romantics admired in Shakespeare. The results are excellent writing; perhaps, the best single piece of prose writing in Russia prior to the 1830's.

Authenticity and historicity are again prominent, with full advantage taken of the depictions of actual historical figures: the Sittsky brothers, the mercenary leader Lisovsky, and even the seventeenth-century Russian author Khvorostinin. In this tale, however, authenticity is not so much a matter of historical personages and scholarly detail as of temporal and local atmosphere. This is a moody tale, full of brooding, and it is apparent that authenticity has become a fully literary quality. The Shakespeare-like settings on the city walls, in the mercenary camp, and in the woods at night are finely rendered, and it is little wonder that Pushkin remarked in an 1825 letter to Bestuzhev: "But the description of the Lithuanian [sic; Lisovsky] camp and the carpenter's conversation with the sentry are charming; the end likewise. Incidentally, extraordinary vivacity is everywhere."[12] Perhaps the setting of the witchcraft scene can serve to illustrate how well authenticity had begun to serve imagination by the time Bestuzhev turned to the writing of *The Traitor:*

Stifling night settled down over the hills of Pereyaslavl; the sky blended into a thunder cloud; the lake was calm in its banks. From time to time a ray of soundless lightning flashes and dies in the dark depths of the waters, marking out on the horizon the peaks of churches and the towers of the town. Heavy clouds, moving forward without wind, are visible in the blue flashing. Everything is still and ghastly, as if nature were mourning before the storm. (I, 136)

The sources for the writing of *The Traitor* are both curious and literarily noteworthy. As has been stated, the facts and events are from Karamzin's *History of the Russian State*, and the structural model, much of the tone, and the types of setting are from Shakespeare. As to this latter source, it is likely that Bestuzhev had both *Othello* and *Hamlet* in mind, but the tale seems to be more of a general response to the Shakespearian manner than a specific utilization of a single drama as a model. It is even possible that Bestuzhev had August Schlegel's famous definition of the Romantic drama in mind while writing his tale, for the way in which he blends his various structural elements gives rise to the suspicion that he was toying with violations of Neoclassical principles. Bestuzhev was also an avid reader of Schiller, and significantly, his story is a severely abbreviated adaptation of Schiller's drama, *Die Räuber* (1781). The basic theme of *The Traitor* is envy and lust for power. This is the prime motivation of Vladimir Sittsky, and it is the mechanism for the conflict between the two brothers, the one a virtuous young leader of his people, the other an evil dissimulator. Envy and lust for power are also key themes of Schiller's drama, and the motivations of Schiller's villain, Franz von Moor, are similar to those revealed by Vladimir:

I will root up from my path whatever obstructs my progress toward becoming the master. — Master I must be, that I may extort by force what I cannot win by affection. (Act I, Scene I)

It is especially the desire for admiration that marks an identity between the characters of Vladimir Sittsky and Franz von Moor.

What is remarkable about Bestuzhev's response to the model of Schiller's drama is that he seems to have based his story exclusively on the Schillerian themes of envy and lust for power and discarded all the other features of the far more complicated German work. It is obvious, for example, that *The Traitor* does not belong to the tradition of "robber" literature, and Bestuzhev departed from Schiller in other respects, too. He dispensed with all but the most essential characters, and thus with the confusing interactions of characters that mark Schiller's drama. This enabled him to avoid also the many intrigues, situations, secondary themes, and scenes (or settings) which make *Die Räuber* so complex. The role of the aged father is absent from the tale (and thus the theme of parricide). Even the prominent role of Schiller's heroine is replaced in *The Traitor* by a few allusions to the object of Vladimir Sittsky's jealousy. The character of the "good" brother has been reduced in favor of Bestuzhev's preoccupation with the psychology of the "evil" hero. This signifies not only a fundamental change of emphasis, but also a disinterest in Schiller's themes of social justice and human freedom associated with the "good" brother, Karl von Moor. Bestuzhev makes no attacks on the church, the nobility, the merchants, or the writer's profession, nor does he preach a moral, as Schiller is so often wont to do. Where Schiller, at the very last moment, adroitly dodges the fact of parricide and fratricide, by introducing substitutes for the act, Bestuzhev meets the fratricide head on by driving his villainous hero to the final — and fully described — murder of his brother. Witchcraft and horror are central to the tale, as they are to the drama, but there are none of the castle accoutrements and ghosts which the Gothic novelists adopted from Schiller's tower. In short, Bestuzhev mercilessly discarded every aspect of *Die Räuber* except the fratricidal conflict. Perhaps this is because he was also responsive to Shakespeare in the writing of *The Traitor*. But given Schiller's own obligations to Shakespeare, this suggestion is moot.

IV   *The Early Tales of Men and Passions: Byron*

Almost all of Bestuzhev's tales could be called "tales of men and passions," for his heroes are all large in their emotions and magnificent in their passions. As Turgenev noted, they have "storms in their souls and fire in their blood." But this second generic category is especially deserving of the title because the conflicts of the heroes of these tales are their dominant factor, as opposed to history, horror, sea adventures, or exoticism. These tales run the gamut of Bestuzhev's career and thus fall into both periods. The features which distinguish them from each other are their different settings and their different combinations of theme and structure. They are united into a single generic category first by the conflicts of their heroes with a crass social milieu and then by their adherence to the Romantic tradition of the society tale, their almost totally consistent concern with the theme of unworthy love, and their contemporariness. Above all, they are the most purely "Byronic" of Bestuzhev's prose tales.

There is little doubt that Byron was the most powerful influence on Russian literature of the 1820's. Byron and Byronism were the rage of the day in both literature and the fashionable poses of young Russians.[13] It is impossible to read through the literary criticism of the men of the 1820's without noting what a high value they placed on the English poet and how thoroughly he stripped them of their usually sharp critical faculties. This is also true of the multitude of Byronesque literary works. Pushkin seems to be the only Russian of the 1820's who soon developed reservations about Byron and began to "outgrow" the Byronic influence. In fact, many of the sharpest criticisms of Pushkin's Romantic verse tales stem from a suspicion that this or that aspect of his writing was not sufficiently Byronic, and *Eugene Onegin* unsettled Pushkin's contemporaries because he had all too obviously not taken Byron seriously in his portrayal of Onegin. No one was more critical of Pushkin in this respect than Bestuzhev and Kondraty Ryleev, and no one was less critical in his response to Byron than Bestuzhev. It may even be said that the respective attitudes of Pushkin and Bestuzhev toward Byron represent two opposite poles of Russian response to Byronism, and here again Bestuzhev proved himself Russia's Romantic extremist.

In Bestuzhev's eyes, Byron was flawless, the paragon of Romantic creativity, the perfect model for any writer who hoped to become worthy of the title Romantic. The way in which his prose tales were influenced by Byron shows that his enthusiasm knew no bounds. He accepted the Byronic hero as the epitome of the Romantic hero, and he found in the Byronic verse tale an ideal model for his own prose tale as a Romantic genre. Byron's verse tales became Bestuzhev's Bible, and under Byron's influence he developed what he considered an appropriate device for the creation of the Russian prose tale — the transposition of the Romantic verse tale into the Russian prose genre.

The Soviet scholar Nikolai I. Mordovchenko has studied this unusual transposition and concluded that there are points of contact in the clear-cut authorial image, the use of metaphors and similes, the lyric digressions, and the methods of characterization.[14] Bestuzhev's narrator is almost always himself — a "stylized Bestuzhev" — and he operates within his tales as effectively as his heroes. In this sense, Byron's infectiously personal mode of narration is indeed an important ingredient of Bestuzhev's transposition. The stylized Bestuzhev does not necessarily resemble Byron, of course, and he is "Byronic" only in the sense that Bestuzhev was himself "Byronic." That is, his narrator is usually a determinedly individualistic Bestuzhev who asserts his own personality, exhibits a proud aloofness from the mundane, succumbs frequently to melodrama, and proclaims his own ideas directly or by making his heroes a mouthpiece. The early stylized Bestuzhev is completely lacking in Byron's greater sophistication, that famed English spleen, and he is sometimes dismayingly subjective and far too prone to hyperbole and declamation.

The same thing may be said of Bestuzhev's methods of characterization. His heroes are thoroughly "Byronic" in character, they are subjectively depicted, their ideals are in conflict with their social milieus. As Mordovchenko has put it, Bestuzhev's heroes inherited from Byron "a deliberate theatricality, and at the same time great passions, strong will, hatred of banality and routine."[15] Bestuzhev was influenced by Kondraty Ryleev in this respect, and this especially set him apart from Pushkin. As Mordovchenko has also noted, "At the time when Pushkin had long since overcome the problem of the subjective-lyric hero of his verse tales . . . Bestuzhev, following Ryleev, ratified in his creativity a particularly subjective-lyric hero."[16] Perhaps even more important, Bestuzhev's Byronic heroes are inevitably positive. They are sometimes villainous, as is the case with Vladimir Sittsky, and they sometimes falter and fail, as with Pravin, the hero of *Fregat "Nadezhda"* ("The Frigate 'Hope' "). But in almost every tale they are indeed passionate, strong-willed, and motivated by a hatred of banality and routine. More often than not they are destroyed by their conflict with society, but they are always fine young men, possessed of lofty ideals, capable of heroic behavior. Their only flaw is their penchant for unworthy society darlings, and this is what makes them vulnerable to the revenge society takes on nonconformists.

Pushkin was very much interested in Bestuzhev's development of the prose tale, and he quickly detected Byron's influence. J. Thomas Shaw has compared Pushkin's short story *The Shot* (1830) with Bestuzhev's *Vecher na bivuake* ("Evening at a Bivouac") and concluded that one reason for the writing of Pushkin's story was to demonstrate "the contrast between the style of his story and of Bestuzhev-Marlinskij's elevated-style heroics and sentiment in a form which Pushkin in 1825 suggested to Bestuzhev himself was proper for a romantic verse tale but not for prose stories."[17] The suggestion to which Shaw refers, and which he quotes, reveals Pushkin's opinion of Bestuzhev's prose tales: "Your *Tournament [at Revel]* is reminiscent of W. Scott's tournaments," he wrote to Bestuzhev. "Away with these furriners, and turn to us Orthodox; and enough of your writing *rapid* tales with romantic transitions — that is all right for a Byronic poem. But a novel requires *chatter:* say everything out plainly."[18]

The suggestion is difficult to interpret, for like so many of the remarks in Pushkin's letters, it points to an idea without spelling it out. But one obvious implication, as indicated by the reference to "*rapid* tales with romantic transitions," is that Pushkin had reservations about the efficacy of the Byronic poem as a structural model for the prose tale. Pushkin apparently had in mind Byron's structural device of quick shifts of subject and setting, either those abrupt transitions which are made without apology to the reader, or those transitions negotiated by a deftly inserted digression. Pushkin had *Tournament at Revel* in mind here, and he mentioned *The Traitor* in this same context. Given the structure of the latter tale, as well as the dominating influences of Shakespeare and Schiller, this was a poor example for Pushkin to choose. But *Tournament at Revel* does indicate many of Bestuzhev's structural obligations to the Byronic verse tale. It shifts scenes and subjects within and across chapter boundaries, makes extensive use of digression, and is indeed a "rapid tale with romantic transitions." Like the Byronic verse tale it employs a variety of narrative techniques — exposition, dialogue, description, and shifts from the main narrator to narration by one or another of the characters. The autonomy of the main narrator is never infringed upon, for even when a character narrates part of the tale, the point of view is clearly Bestuzhev's. And that point of view is consistently subjective.

The influence of Byron — the transposition of the Byronic verse tale into the Russian prose tale — would seem to contain three elements: a narrative method (the stylized Bestuzhev), a type of hero, and a structural model. But the process of the transposition is a complex one, and none of these three elements should be understood as a matter of simple adaptation. Bestuzhev's enthusiasm gave him a view of Byron which is far removed from the Byron known in English literature, and the demands of his chosen genre prevented him from honoring his view as closely as he might have wished. As has been pointed out, the narrator of Bestuzhev's tale is in no way like Byron himself. The narrator's *manner* is Byronic in that he is "subjective-lyric," highly individualistic, and does not hesitate to play a role in the tales. But the personality is Bestuzhev's own. The same thing is true of Bestuzhev's "Byronic" heroes, and this is why they must be referred to in quotes. They are *positive* heroes, without sophistication, frequently without depth, and too often so stereotyped as to become caricatures of the Byronic hero. This is indicated by Bestuzhev's penchant for false heroics and affected speech, and these features are underscored by the use of rhetoric, declamation, and hyperbole far in excess of Byron. To put it plainly, Bestuzhev's heroes are not like Childe Harold, Don Juan, or Manfred; they are Bestuzhev's own creations influenced by his own extreme interpretation of what a Byronic hero should be.

The transposition is an undeniable fact, and it must be admitted that it is an ingenious device; but if the method is clear, the result is not. It is possible to isolate individual instances of the transposition in the structural elements of most of Bestuzhev's tales, but no single tale can be labeled a Byronic verse tale in a Russian prose form. Nor are the reasons for this difficult to find. The tales are influenced not only by Byron, but also by Karamzin, Scott, and the Gothic novel. Some tales are obviously formed on the basis of different models — *The Traitor,* for example. And although Karamzin, Scott, the Gothic novelists, Shakespeare, and Schiller are the dominant influences on the development of Bestuzhev's prose tale, there are also indications of influence by Chateaubriand and Constant, Florian, Madame Genlis, and even Washington Irving.[19] Given Bestuzhev's erudition in his own literature, it is probable that he was influenced by the verse models of Zhukovsky, Pushkin, Baratynsky, Ryleev, to say nothing of the eighteenth-century authors of longer verse works. And finally, while it is evident the transposition was deliberate, the process inevitably had, as a built-in factor, a tendency to remove the two genres one from another. Influences are always important and interesting, and Bestuzhev was especially dependent, as are all originators of new literary traditions, but he was too independent to confine himself strictly to his models.

The tales of men and passions abound with a display of Romantic emotion in the predicaments of young idealists, and the plot situations reveal their nature most readily. *Noch' na korable* ("Night on a Ship," 1822) is a young Scottish officer's story of the tragic consequences of his love for an unworthy society belle. Years after she has broken his heart, she dies unloved and unwanted. *Roman v semi pis'makh* ("A Romance in Seven Letters," 1824) is a brief epistolary tale in which a young man tells of his duel over a beautiful woman. He has killed his rival in a jealous rage, and now realizes the woman did not love him. *Chasy i zerkalo* ("The Clock and the Mirror," 1832) is another guard officer's story of an unworthy woman. He has returned to visit her in St. Petersburg, where he enjoys his revenge: the clock ticks away her wasted years and the mirror before which she primps herself reveals the signs of approaching age.

To a dismaying degree the tales of this category are remarkable for their literary naïveté. In *A Romance in Seven Letters* the hero is enraptured by his darling, "Ah, how dear she is, George, how dear she is!" In his final letter he expresses his remorse with unalleviated passion: "I killed him, I killed this noble, magnanimous man!" and: "Why are we not at war . . . why do they not shoot me!" Fortunately, this penchant for false heroics and extraordinary passions is brought under control in the later tales of men and passions. *Ispytanie* ("The Test," 1830) is a humorous tale: the story of two frivolous hussars who compete for the hand of a beautiful woman and outsmart themselves in a "test" of her constancy. After a series of wittily handled adventures, they are stopped short of settling their differences in a duel. The tale is filled with racy dialogue, humorous digressions, and fine parodies of the styles of Bestuzhev's contemporaries, including Pushkin.

The best of the early tales of men and passions are *Evening at a Bivouac* and *Vtoroy vecher na bivuake* ("An Evening at a Bivouac" and "A Second Evening at a Bivouac," both 1823). The "bivouac" or "hussar" tales are heavily stamped with the influence of Byron, particularly in their narration and the characterization of the heroes, but they depart completely from the Byronic structural model: they are anecdotal in structure, with a setting in military bivouacs during the War of 1812. If they are still affected by false heroics and hyperbole, their structure is sophisticated, and they are distinguished by a quick-paced witty dialogue.The tales are identical in theme and structure, as well as by characters.

An Evening at a Bivouac begins with a description of a hussar bivouac, followed quickly by the arrival of the swaggering cuirassier Prince Olsky, whose bantering manner rouses the tired hussars to a duel of witty repartée. In a smooth transition from snappy dialogue to storytelling, Prince Olsky boasts of a night on which he paid a courtesy call to the French camp in search of good champagne and company. This and an amusing second anecdote, told by the young hussar Lidin, pave the way for a serious story told by Colonel Mechin — the story of an idealistic young hussar, Mechin himself, for a frivolous young society woman. According to his story, Mechin had fallen in love with Sofia, the belle of St. Petersburg society. When an envious rival makes a joke at Sofia's expense, Mechin challenges him to a duel. Gravely wounded before he can take his own shot, Mechin recovers many weeks later to discover that Sofia has become engaged to the very man from whom he had tried to defend her honor. Enraged by this turn of affairs, he swears to kill his rival — he is still due his shot — but is saved from this rash action by his friend Vladov, who has him sent from the capital. Years later he again encounters Sofia at a Caucasian watering spa. Abandoned by her uncouth husband and now dying of consumption, she is comforted in her last hours by the staunch hussar.

The second hussar story is in every way the same. Mechin and his hussars are again gathered around the campfire, again they are roused to a biting round of banter, and again there is a deft transition to the telling of two humorous anecdotes, followed by another sad story of unworthy love told by Mechin. This time the story is about Mechin's friend Vladov. Relating how he was also once betrayed by a faithless woman, Vladov had told Mechin of his disillusionment with love and with society, and he predicts his own death in battle. In the end, exactly as Vladov had predicted, Mechin finds him dying on a battlefield: " 'Don't cry,' he continued, gasping painfully, 'Don't pity me, because I regret only the friendships I have had on this earth. I was unable to live, and that is why I am able to die. . . . Russia, my homeland!' he cried, 'Mechin, forgive. . . .' " (I, 66)

As these lines indicate, false heroics are indeed a prominent feature of the hussar stories. And although they are the only significant shortcoming of the two works, they are sufficiently prominent to require attention, particularly for what they show about Bestuzhev's Byronic characters. Mechin, for example, is undeniably a positive hero. His two stories show him to be possessed of lofty ideals, especially his ideal of true love, and the attitude of his hussars toward him shows that he is highly admired for his fortitude, his modesty, and his courage in battle. Like every good Byronic hero, he has a mysterious past, a past which is revealed to be both sad and tragic. Although by 1812 he has become a disciplined leader of men, able to look thoughtfully and calmly at his past, in his youth he had been impetuous and passionate. Even now, the narrator gives us to understand, his cool image of a military commander hides deep emotions and an impulsive will. This last quality is fully exposed by the passion of his words when he relates his reaction to Sofia's treachery: "Fury and revenge, like lightning, flooded my blood. I swore to shoot him, according to the code of the duel (I was still due my shot at him), so that the crafty woman would not be able to triumph with him. . . . My friends, do you know what the thirst for blood and revenge is like? I tasted it on that terrible night!" The same false heroics can be noted in his account of a miraculous escape from death in battle: "Providence . . . spared me from death on the banks of the Danube to serve my fatherland a bit longer — the bullet smashed against Sofia's portrait-medallion. . . ." It can be detected even more clearly in the words with which Mechin describes Sofia's death: "It is terrible to even recall it . . . Sofia died in my arms!" (I, 52, 53, 54)

What saves the two hussar stories from artistic disaster is their efficient structure. The stories are tight and compact, and their brevity, combined with the adept and consistent transitions from opening description to witty banter to humorous anecdotes to the concluding stories which contrast very well with the foregoing passages, make them highly effective in narrative manner. The initial humor contrasts admirably with the serious stories on the theme of unworthy love, and all of this is wrapped in the lively atmosphere of the hussar bivouac. The structure permits Bestuzhev not only to indulge in false heroics and affected sentiments, but to display one of his finest talents — his ability to handle swift, witty dialogue. In fact, the dialogue and anecdotes are just as important to the stories as the structure. D. S. Mirsky had perhaps these stories in mind when when he observed that while Bestuzhev's "superficially passionate heroes, with their Byronic pose, are rather cheap," his dialogue "is especially brilliant, a constant battledore and shuttlecock of pithy epigram and witty repartée."[20] Bestuzhev's characters are given to such remarks as "Even you hussars proved today that you don't wear your mentique on your right shoulder," a hint that since their hussar jackets had been thrown back, they must have used their sword arms well. When Prince Olsky is addressed, "I hear you, Your Radiance," he retorts, "My Radiance doesn't hear or listen to a thing until he's downed a bit of glint wine, without which he is neither radiant nor dark," and his wit wins him his drink. The same character begins his anecdote with the boastful remark that "My hunger increased all the more since from the French line could be heard the harmonious mooing of oxen — answered by the plaintive echo of my own empty belly." When the cynical hussar Nichtovich remarks about his boastful anecdote, "Wasn't that in print somewhere?" Olsky retorts, "If it were in print, it would have to be news to you!" And when the hussar persists, asking, "And after what affair did it happen?" Olsky silences him for good with the retort, "After the same one in which you were wounded in the *heel*." When Mechin raves over his love for Sofia, Vladov subdues him with the query, "What makes you so sure the princess is sighing from love, and not from a tight corset?"[21]

The last, the best, and the most sophisticated of the tales of men and passions is *The Test,* written in 1830 and published that same year in *Son of the Fatherland* and *Northern Archive.* Although it belongs to the period of the 1830's, it may be treated usefully under its generic category as a continuation of the Byronic tales. The tale is very much like its generic predecessors in that it focuses on a main character, a beautiful heroine, and a high society milieu. Society is shown to be if not crass, then superficial and ridiculous, and the hero's ideals are dramatized in contrast to society's standards. The tale contains both serious and sarcastic commentaries on society. Where the tale differs from its predecessors is in its length and complexity — it is thus a culmination as well as a continuation of the category — and in the fact that it is a humorous work with a happy ending. At first glance the humorous, even comical, quality of the tale would seem to make it very much unlike the previous tales of tragically unrequited love, but to so ignore its serious social intent would be to fail to appreciate it as what it is — a serious Byronic treatment of the same problems encountered in the hussar tales.

The situation and intrigue of *The Test* are straightforward. Valerian Strelinsky and Nikolay Gremin are two hussars stationed near Kiev. As the tale opens, Gremin is entertaining a party of hussars in his bachelor quarters. Strelinsky arrives on his way to St. Petersburg, and following a quick round of banter and puns, he is called aside by Gremin, who explains his love for Alina, a rich, beautiful widow, and states the tale's situation in a single succinct request: ". . . test Alina's constancy. You are young and wealthy, you are charming and adroit — in a word, no one can lose money on purpose better than you and no one can win a heart with such foolish ardor. Give me your word — and go to it!"

Given such a promising situation, it is a foregone conclusion that Strelinsky, in testing Alina's love for Gremin, will himself fall under her spell. Contriving to meet her at a masked ball in the disguise of a "Don Alonzo," he charms her completely and is himself charmed into falling in love with her. Following a long interlude of doubt, Strelinsky surrenders to his feeling and proposes. Alina, however, senses her suitor's doubts and postpones her acceptance. At this point Gremin arrives, and although it is made clear that he has meanwhile fallen in love with Strelinsky's younger sister Olga, he is chagrined at his friend's treachery and challenges him to a duel. The two friendly foes are thus faced with a dilemma. Strelinsky's better self tells him that Alina truly loves him, yet he still doubts her and feels guilty toward his friend. Gremin realizes he has made too much of Alina's feelings for him, he knows he now loves Olga instead, but his pride has been offended. Both men understand they are about to fight a duel which has no meaning, but neither is willing to swallow his pride. Fortunately, the two hussars are prevented from transforming their ridiculous test into a tragedy. Olga arrives at the scene of the duel, chastises the antagonists, and reconciles them. Embarrassed by the knowledge that they outsmarted themselves, each prepares to marry the lady of his choice.

If the tale's situation is simple, however, its form and structure are not. There are a great many humorous twists and turns in the plot which provide exciting entertainment. Suspense is created by putting the outcome in doubt, by changing scenes and subjects at critical moments, and even by witholding "Don Alonzo's" identity for almost three chapters. (Is it Gremin or Strelinsky who has won Alina's heart?) The author's talent for handling dialogue — his adroit repartée and puns — is put to its finest use, particularly in the opening scene where Strelinsky delivers a running commentary on each of the assembled hussars lying on and under the table in a drunken stupor, and also in the scene of the masked ball where the hero carries on a duel of wits with the heroine. In the latter scene the dialogue is at its best, as can be seen in the pace of the banter: each witticism is broken off and rejoined by the sequences of the dance, thus giving a swing to several pages of smooth, graceful, and witty chatter.

Equally important to the tale's structure are the author's many expositions and digressions. Chapter Two, for example, is a colorful digression on the charm of St. Petersburg and is a prose version of Byron's treatment of the "Palmyra of the North" in *Don Juan*. Chapter Three begins with a lively description of a society ball and is a parody of similar descriptions in Pushkin's *Eugene Onegin* and Baratynsky's Romantic verse tale *The Ball* — both of which were first published together in *The Polar Star*. The humorous opening description of a bachelor officer's quarters is well handled, as is the authorial exposition on the art of the duel. Worked adroitly into this complex structure are a number of traditional Romantic scenes: not only the ball and the duel, but the proposal, the enraged confrontation between honorable antagonists, the heroine's boudoir, the social whirl, the meeting between lovers (Gremin and Olga) at the piano, and others.

Despite the tale's humorous nature, it does have, as previously stated, a serious intent. It should not be missed, for example, that the tale begins on St. Nicholas Day at an estate "not far from Kiev" — a bit of covert language signifying the Davydov-Raevsky estate Kamenka, where the Decembrists of the Southern Society held their meetings in the early 1820's. Moreover, although the hussars present are described in comical terms, it is quite likely that their characteristics are those of selected Southern Decembrists. Above all, the serious social commentaries of the author and the serious discussions between Strelinsky and Alina are reaffirmations of Bestuzhev's own Decembrist ideals.

It is relevant, for example, that beneath his pose of flippancy, Strelinsky dreams of a deeply idealistic life of service to the Russian people. In the narrator's words: "While his friends and comrades considered him a mere wastrel, concerned only with squandering his income, he secretly made all necessary sacrifices for the improvement of the condition of his peasants, who like most manor people had been left to him half ruined economically and half depraved morally." This is the crux of the hero's doubts about Alina, for having determined to devote his life to the betterment of his peasants, he is reluctant to tie himself to someone who may be little more than a society darling. He need not have worried, of course, for Alina proves also to be a person of depth. She shares his ideals and even deplores the same general slavery to French culture that Bestuzhev decried in his earlier "Glances" at Russian literature.

Thus, the tale's situation involves not only the question of mutual trust in the love intrigue between hero and heroine, but also the development of mutual respect and a shared devotion to important social aims. In this way, the love intrigue becomes a vehicle for the tale's social purpose, a purpose disguised by the prominence of the humor. Very apparently, then, the same social concerns expressed in the early tales of men and passions are expressed again in this most sophisticated tale of the category. Only after Strelinsky comes to realize that Alina is not a mere socialite, and she receives proof that he is not a young fop of the age, is the love intrigue resolved. In retrospect, many of their proclamations of social ideals seem pompous — discussions of economic problems on a moonlit night — but the tale is one of Bestuzhev's most important statements of his Decembrist beliefs.

Three things may be reiterated by way of a summation of the nature of Bestuzhev's prose tales of the early period. It is first of all evident that while none of the early tales reaches a high level of literary value, and some are unsophisticated to a dismaying degree, Bestuzhev was obviously mastering techniques and devices which lent great impetus to his growing skill as a writer. It is a long way from the awkwardness of the castle tales to the promise of *The Traitor* and the proficiency of the hussar stories.

It is also clear that the means by which he devised and then developed his chosen genre is the result of careful thought. He freely used the scant tradition of his own nation's literature and was eagerly responsive to the models of European writers. The Karamzin example and the transposition of the Byronic verse tale were the starting point, while to this basic method were added the lessons learned from Scott, the Gothic novel, Shakespeare, and Schiller. It is curious that while his criticism and theory were influenced most by German Romantic Idealism, he turned mainly to English literature for his literary experience. His willingness to remain so responsive to external models was tempered by his equal willingness to experiment. The process of his adaptation of the themes and techniques of others reveals not only a literary education, but also a sense for the organic development of his own talents and literary abilities.

And finally, it is evident that one of Bestuzhev's assets as a writer, his most original talent, was his capacity for an almost scholarly approach to literature. His knowledge of his subject matter, be it a historical period, a style of architecture, or a geographic area, lent his tales a quality unknown to any other writer of his time. This feature is useless in and of itself, but he made it into a literary value and entertained his readers with an imaginative use of the most fascinating details. The technique of saturation survived throughout his career and became one of the reasons for his great popularity as the ultra-Romantic writer of the 1830's — Alexander Marlinsky.

CHAPTER 4

Alexander Marlinsky: The Extravagant Prose — 1830-37

THE return of Alexander Bestuzhev to an active literary career under the name Alexander Marlinsky was met with heartily if privately expressed relief, and the event was probably interpreted as a harbinger of imminent political change. Far off in Siberia the exiled Decembrist Küchelbecker received a copy of Marlinsky's new tale of men and passions, *The Test*, and he noted in his diary: "There is so much life, intellect, action, and feeling in it that it may be reckoned without the least doubt among the finest prose tales in our language. . . . God bless whoever spared this man of talent for our fatherland! *Sapienti sat.*"[1]

As it turned out, the event did not presage any liberalization of the regime of Nicholas I, but it was indeed a boon for Russian literature. It announced a new and relatively high standard of Russian prose writing, and it is apparent that Alexander Marlinsky was a far better writer than his predecessor. His tales of the second period are longer, revealing a confident ability to control form and structure. The mature prose tales are characterized by a wide variety of stylistic manners — exposition, digression, dialogue, descriptive passages, direct and indirect narrative — and they are remarkable for the myriads of stylistic devices that made the style known as Marlinism so powerful in its effect on the reader of the 1830's. Alexander Marlinsky was obviously his own writer, no longer dependent on external models. This is the period of a skilled literary craftsman.

I *The Sea Stories*

Marlinsky wrote two fine tales of men and passions in the 1830's — *The Test* and *The Clock and the Mirror* — and both tales are closely related to the third generic category, the sea stories. There are three sea stories — *Leitenant Belozor* ("Lieutenant Belozor," 1831), *Fregat "Nadezhda"* ("The Frigate 'Hope,'" 1832), and

Morekhod Nikitin ("Merchant Sailor Nikitin," 1834) — and the first two are tales of impetuous men in conflict with society. It was not by chance that Marlinsky became the first Russian author of naval adventures. He was fascinated by the sea, and his seascapes are a prominent feature of many of his tales and essays. "He was unable to speak tranquilly about the sea," noted Nikolay A. Kotlyarevsky, "and beneath his pen a seascape was involuntarily transformed into a lyric elocution."[2]

In his youth Marlinsky wanted to become a naval officer. His brothers Nikolay and Mikhail were naval officers, and the former was the author of sea stories. During his teens Marlinsky spent summers at sea with Nikolay and gained a proficient technical knowledge of ships. When Nikolay Polevoy expressed surprise at the appearance of a type of tale he had not expected from Marlinsky, the author commented in a letter of 1833: "Do not be surprised that I know naval technology — I am a sailor born and a sailor bred. The sea has been my passion, ships my vice, and although I never served with the fleet, I will not yield place in any way to a genuine sailor, even in the minute details of ship-building. There was a time when I hungered for service with the fleet, but for all that I prefer a horse to a ship — at least one can abandon the former."[3]

Marlinsky's three sea stories, all lengthy, are united into a single generic category by their sea setting and their use of richly authentic naval language, including a healthy dose of sailor's jargon. With the exception, perhaps, of *The Frigate "Hope"*, they are not the best of Marlinsky's works, but they are well-done tales of exciting adventure and became very popular. Belinsky, for example, declared that "for me [Marlinsky's] best tales are easily *The Test* and *Lieutenant Belozor* — one can admire his talent without reservation, for he is in his proper element in them."[4]

The authenticity of technical terms and jargon is without doubt the most striking feature of the sea stories. In *Lieutenant Belozor* the hero's ship is described in minute detail, with all the regalia of its topmasts and yardarms, storm sails, gutters, rigging, admiral's main-mast, and spars. The ships make such maneuvers as "to come up to the fleet in full sail," and orders are given to "haul into the line and cast anchor to the flagship's portside." Such terms are encountered as reserve pumps, flares, north-north-west, flag, signals, and signal book. Passing ships are called "gentlemen" in sailor's slang, and in one instance it is mentioned that "the commands rigged their sails in what is called *in honor*." Once a sailor shouts in English: "Don't skid away, my boys! Hard aport and close up to the wind!" The same conscientiously careful and colorfully colloquial naval language is a dominant feature of the other two sea stories.

Merchant Sailor Nikitin is saturated with such English terms as "hot-pressed," "man-of-war," "boat-ahoo! strike your colors," "down with your rags!" "put the helm up, damn!" "strike, or I'll run over and sink you!" and "god damn your eyes! you scoundrels, ruffians, and barbed dogs!" English terms are also given in Cyrillic transcription, such as *kutter, shkiper, yanki, blokshif, kapery i kreysery, flagman, boy, puding i grog,* and *angliyskie goddemy.* Betraying his interest in language for its own sake, Marlinsky explains that an East Indies ship is "an 'Indianen' [sic], as the English say." In a footnote to one still fairly new British expression, Marlinsky observes: "The English call the North-Americans Yankee as a means of ridicule." Authentic terms are so profuse in the sea stories, and the device of saturating whole passages with technical terminology and jargon is so pronounced a feature, that it must be concluded once again Marlinsky's first love was for languages. And he succeeded again in making the device an entertaining feature, one that must have fascinated Russian readers of the 1830's.

The best of Marlinsky's sea tales is *The Frigate "Hope",* which illustrates most readily the adventure tale qualities of this generic category. Captain-Lieutenant Ilya Petrovich Pravin is the captain of the finest ship in the Russian fleet, the "Hope." He is adored by his sailors, respected by his officers, and known even to Tsar Nicholas for his devotion to ship, duty, and honor. Beneath his staunch, practical exterior, however, he is an idealist and a dreamer — not very different from Colonel Mechin of the hussar stories — and he is also completely naïve with regard to hypocritical St. Petersburg society. "He knew well the nature of the sea," Marlinsky observes, "but where could he have learned the nature of men?" Chosen by highest authority to command a somehow important but never fully explained voyage to the Mediterranean, Pravin looks forward, in the year 1829, to a fine and honorable career. At just this critical juncture of his life Pravin meets and falls in love with Vera, the wife of an elderly court official, Prince Pyotr***.

At first it seems that his sense of duty will vanquish his passion. Led to believe that Vera has been toying with his emotions, he buries himself in the difficult technical preparations for the voyage. He encounters Vera alone one day, however, and upon learning that his suspicions were unfounded, makes an emotional declaration of love.

On the eve of departure, the "Hope" is boarded by Prince Pyotr and Vera, who has used her husband's influence to arrange a pleasure trip to England. The inexperienced Pravin neglects his duty and gives himself over to an affair with Vera. And when she departs the ship in Plymouth harbor, he is unable to resist the demands of his passion. Even though a storm is rising, and his second officer begs him to stay with the "Hope", he goes ashore for one last rendezvous with the woman he loves.

The following morning, after a night in Vera's boudoir, the lovers are discovered by Prince Pyotr, and Pravin is numbed by the realization he has compromised his beloved. Worse yet, at this moment Pravin learns his ship has been struck by the storm. Torn between his commitment to Vera and his duty to the "Hope," he is unable to act. Only when it is too late, does he attempt to return to his ship. He is injured in the attempt and, tormented by the knowledge of his failure to both Vera and the ship, dies in disgrace.

The Frigate "Hope" provides a good illustration of the nature of Marlinsky's mature prose tales. Primarily an exciting adventure tale, its action-packed story can be ranked with the best adventure tales of Scott, Cooper, Hugo, and Dumas, père. Within another decade this type of literary endeavor no longer appealed to the sophisticated Russian reader, but tales such as *The Frigate "Hope"* are the reason for Marlinsky remaining a popular writer well into the twentieth century. The love story, the exciting events, the glamor of the sea, the tragedy of a brave hero's failure to meet a challenge to his manhood, the fascinatingly technical descriptions of ships — these features have had a lasting and powerful effect on the imagination of young readers.

The tale is also notable for its structural complexity, a consistent quality of the mature tales. The main narrator is still that stylized Byronic narrator, but point of view is varied by a number of devices which enable the characters to conduct parts of the narrative. We learn a great deal about Pravin and are given an insight into Vera's personality by her letters to a friend; Pravin's lofty ideals and passionate character emerge from his letters to his best friend aboard the "Hope." Point of view is varied further by dialogue, and we gain a more objective view of the love situation from the pungent remarks of a sarcastic ship's doctor. The plot is relieved and enhanced by descriptive passages, digressions, and the seascapes. The aftermath of the tragedy at sea is conveyed in an understated postscript to the tale, half of which shows that Vera was able to return unaffected to her position in St. Petersburg society, the other half being a curious news story in *The Northern Bee* about the "Hope's" return to her home port. The tale is marked by *literaturnost'* — the Russian art of literary allusion — and many of these allusions, including the news story, indicate that the tale is a thinly disguised allegory of Marlinsky's own fate in the Decembrist conspiracy.[5] The main narrative, the epistolary interludes, the dialogue, the descriptive and expository passages, and the literary allusions — all reinforced by deftly inserted witticisms — make this tale complex, variegated, and entertaining. Best of all, these diverse elements are blended organically into a single, graceful literary work which is far superior to the awkward experiments of the early period.

II   *The Tales of Horror: Mrs. Radcliffe*

Just as well written are the three tales of horror which make up the fourth generic category: *Vecher na kavkazskikh vodakh v 1824 godu* ("An Evening at a Caucasian Spa in 1824," 1830), including an addendum entitled *Sledstvie vechera na kavkazskikh vodakh v 1824 godu* ("A Sequel to an Evening at a Caucasian Spa in 1824"); *Strashnoe gadanie: Rasskaz* ("The Terrible Divination: A Story," 1830); and *Latnik: Rasskaz partizanskogo ofitsera* ("The Cuirassier: A Partisan Officer's Story," 1831). The first and last of these tales are, like the earlier hussar stories, anecdotal in structure. All three tales are ventures into Russian folklore. Marlinsky was always interested in the supernatural as a source of literary themes and as an enticing Romantic tradition. Many of his early tales contain references to Mrs. Radcliffe, and his castle tales were a response to the Gothic novel. By 1825 he had achieved an estimable proficiency in the conveyance of sweet terror, as indicated by *The Traitor*. Nevertheless, it is apparent that in the 1820's Marlinsky had not yet detected the delicate devices of the Gothic novel, for his early attempts at the creation of horror are direct, and thus ineffective. This bluntness of technique is absent from the mature tales of horror, and it is evident Marlinsky learned a great deal about Gothic methods in the interim.

Curiously, it was not from the models of Mrs. Radcliffe that Marlinsky learned Gothic techniques, but from Walter Scott. In 1824 Scott wrote a "Prefatory Memoir to the Novels of Mrs. Ann Radcliffe" in which he analyzed the methods of a woman and a genre he admired. The memoir was published in Russian in 1826.[6] Marlinsky undoubtedly read at least the Russian version, for he

restated some of Scott's ideas in his own comments on the supernatural as a literary subject. The chief assumption of Scott's view of
the Gothic novel is that the reader of his time was too sophisticated
to be affected by a straightforward treatment of horror and too
rational to accept unexplained supernatural events. "The public of
the current day," he noted, "deals . . . rigidly in moving for a *quo
warranto* to compel an explanation from the story-teller, and the
author must either at once represent the knot as worthy of being
severed by supernatural aid, and bring on the stage his actual fiend
or ghost, or, like Mrs. Radcliffe, explain by natural agency the whole
marvels of his means." The Gothic novelist is faced with a dilemma,
for his materials are incredible and his reader a skeptic: "In the age
of universal credibility, we must own it would require, at the present
day, the support of the highest powers, to save the supernatural from
slipping into the ludicrous." In short, there is a fine line between
credible terror and ridiculous incredibility, and Scott summed up
this most crucial esthetic problem of the Gothic novel in Napoleon's
observation that "there is but one step betwixt the sublime and the
ridiculous."[7]

According to Scott, writers had attempted to deal with this
problem in two contrary ways: those who like Horace Walpole
"compound betwixt ancient faith and modern incredulity . . .
without giving a defined or absolute opinion;" those who like Mrs.
Radcliffe imposed the rule that "all circumstances of her narrative,
however mysterious, and apparently superhuman, were to be accounted for on natural principles, at the winding up of the story." In
Scott's opinion, the first class of writers had merely "eliminated the
obstacle without solving the problem," and the second had achieved
only partial success in the achievement of credibility. Mrs. Radcliffe,
for example, was "more successful in exciting interest and apprehen-
sions than in giving either interest or dignity of explanation to the
means she has made use of." That is, her rational explanations of
supernatural events "at the winding up of the story" ruined the
effect of all that had gone before. The Gothic novelist cannot be
direct in manner. In all other respects, however, Mrs. Radcliffe's
novels were successful, and Scott especially liked two of the keys she
had discovered to the creation of genuine terror: the conveyance of a
sense of guilt and the building up of suspense. Her novels are good
because "the materials . . . and the means employed in conducting
the narrative, are all selected with a view to the author's primary object, of moving the reader by ideas of impending danger, hidden

guilt, supernatural visitings — by all that is terrible, in short, combined with much that is wonderful." They are all the better because "to break off the narrative, when it seemed at the point of becoming most interesting — to extinguish a lamp when a parchment ought to have been read, to exhibit shadowy forms and half-heard sounds of woe, were resources which Mrs. Radcliffe has employed with more effect than any other writer of romance."[8]

Marlinsky must have read Scott very carefully, for his best tale of horror, *The Cuirassier,* observes each of the methods which Scott praised in Mrs. Radcliffe's novels, and it solves the crucial problem of credibility by providing natural explanations of supernatural events in a convincing way. *The Cuirassier* is in fact one of the best of Marlinsky's prose tales and his most sophisticated narrative. Told in a single narrative body, without division into chapters, it consists of two similar anecdotes enlarged into full stories and merged with a main narrative body to form a graceful literary unity. The two frame stories are merged with and interrupted by events of the main narrative and alternate with one another to achieve interruption at a suspenseful moment. This device of alternation facilitates a natural explanation to each story at its "winding up," with the explanations negotiated so naturally and with such an adroit contrast in point of view that they add to, rather than detract from, the feeling of horror.

The main narrator of *The Cuirassier* is a hussar commander of a partisan detachment in 1812, and his story begins with an account of a fierce skirmish in which the hussars are rallied to victory by a Russian cuirassier, who plunges into the midst of the enemy and hacks the unit's commander to pieces. The cuirassier then vanishes, leaving the hussars horrified by his atrocity. When they settle down to their evening bivouac in a deserted manor house, their mood prompts the telling of the two frame stories.

The first story, told by an old serf-retainer, is the legend of the Glinsky manor. At one time the household had rung with happiness, but then, in quick succession, word was received that the daughter's — Felicia's — fiancé had died, Felicia was obliged to marry an avaricious neighbor, Ostrolensky the father died, and Felicia was driven to death by her cruel husband. Shortly before her death Felicia had been seen in the garden with a black horseman, and on the eve of her death she had been overheard conversing with an uncanny presence. Now the Glinsky manor is believed to be occupied by terrible dark powers.

The second story, told by the brooding hussar Zarnitsky, is the legend of the manor of Shuran, once dominated by Zarnitsky's grandfather, the cruel tyrant Prince K. When the daughter, Liza, eloped with her tutor, Bayanov, the old man captured and imprisoned them. Eventually Liza went insane, and it was believed that the mysterious screams of a young man locked in a dungeon were connected with Prince K.'s own insanity and death. In his childhood, Zarnitsky was fascinated by the legend of Shuran, and when he grew up, he decided to dispel its mystery. Despite his dread, he explores the manor, finds a secret passage to a tower, and climbs the stairs. There, before his eyes, beyond doubt, stands the martyred Liza, still young and beautiful.

At this moment Zarnitsky's narrative is interrupted by the reappearance of the cuirassier. He gazes at the portrait of Felicia on the wall, proclaims he has avenged her, and falls into a faint. The hussars realize he is the supposedly deceased fiancé, and in the morning he retells the old serf's story from his own point of view, thus resolving the mystery. The news of his death had been falsified by Ostrolensky with a forged letter, and he was the black horseman in the garden, who had come to curse Felicia for betraying him. He soon learned of Ostrolensky's treachery, however, and the voices heard on the eve of Felicia's death had been the lovers' reconciliation. Ostrolensky had run off to Paris and come back to Russia as a renegade in Napoleon's army: the cuirassier had finally caught up with his enemy that day. It is *à propos* of this revelation that the mystery of Shuran is also explained. For in a now calm and matter-of-fact tone, Zarnitsky reveals that the girl in the tower was the daughter of Liza and Bayanov. Ending his story with a confession of unrequited love for the girl explains his obsession with the legend of Shuran. The tale ends with the death of the cuirassier, and the hussars prepare for another day in battle.

In writing *The Cuirassier*, Marlinsky used three of Scott's suggestions on the esthetics of horror tales. It is significant, for example, that his tale is marked by a careful selection of materials and narrative method aimed at "moving the reader by ideas of impending danger, hidden guilt, supernatural visitings." The mysterious black horseman, the voices on the eve of Felicia's death, the uncanny resurrection of the beautiful Liza, and the aura surrounding the legends of the Glinsky manor and Shuran — these ideas do indeed convey a sense of impending danger. Feelings of guilt are also present in the tale: Zarnitsky's brooding character, his obsession with Shuran, and the hint of incest implied by his love for his cousin; the cuirassier's terrible vengeance and his guilt for tormenting Felicia unjustly. Marlinsky treats these aspects of the tale skillfully and he also reveals an expertise at selecting details for their effect on the reader's imagination. When Zarnitsky approaches Shuran, he perceives certain external objects which have a specific effect on his nerves and create a feeling of "impending danger." His way through the yard is hindered by startled frogs in the grass, and the fallen porch reminds him of his childhood dread: " . . . fantastic beings brushed me with familiar wings, and that former feeling of sweet terror clenched my breast. I stood once again a schoolboy before an ancient castle." When he enters the house, his feeling of dread is heightened by the sight of such objects as scattered furniture, a spider web, green bronze door hinges and rusted fastenings, hanging wallpaper, and streams of rain marks down the walls. A simile is drawn between "bats with membraneous wings" and "the butterflies of ruined edifices," and this simile is effective in imparting the feeling, as opposed to the embodiment, of dread. The thought that "in every quiver of the wallpaper I seemed to hear the moan of a dying victim" is a well-contrived exhibition of those "shadowy forms and half-heard sounds of woe" which Scott singled out as one of Mrs. Radcliffe's techniques. Above all, the passage shows that Marlinsky had realized one of the most important things about the Gothic technique: that objects — accoutrement — are chosen not for their own sake, but for their power to evoke a feeling of the supernatural.

Scott's recommendation that the narrative be interrupted "when it seemed at the point of becoming most interesting" was also followed carefully in the writing of Marlinsky's tale. The mystery of the Glinsky manor, first represented in the old serf's story, is not resolved until almost the end of the tale, when the cuirassier explains the mysterious and apparently superhuman circumstances of the legend. The interruption of Zarnitsky's story is even more abrupt, and here the problem of suspense is well handled. The effect of the manor house on Zarnitsky's overwrought imagination is culminated in Zarnitsky's digression to explain his obsession with the legend of the beautiful Liza. This is followed by an increase of suspense as Zarnitsky approaches the tower, and then the climax, the discovery of the girl. If Marlinsky had added anything at this point, or attempted to increase a tension that had already hit its peak, he would have destroyed his effect. Once the narrative has been interrupted, however, and attention has been drawn back to the legend of the

Glinsky manor, Zarnitsky is able to explain his mystery in a calm tone which contrasts and enhances, rather than destroys, the suspense.

The way in which Marlinsky chose to handle suspense shows also that he devoted thought to Scott's third point — the danger that the accounting of "all circumstances of the narrative . . . at the winding up of the story" would annoy, rather than satisfy. Marlinsky handled his explanations of natural causes for supposedly supernatural events with considerable skill. The explanations clear up the mysteries by natural means but leave an aftermath effect: they preserve the aura of the supernatural and invoke a feeling of lingering dread. This is due in part to the mood of the narrators themselves, for the cuirassier explains the mystery of the Glinsky manor in a state of frenzy, while Zarnitsky's matter-of-fact resolution accentuates his brooding personality. Moreover, the explanations are not only removed from the mysteries by prolonged intervening events, but they are given from a strikingly different point of view. Marlinsky found his solution to the problem of credibility in the very method of narration, exploiting this solution efficiently. The mystery of the Glinsky manor is narrated by a serf, a barely literate and highly superstitious old man who does not comprehend the ways of the nobility, while the explanation is provided by the cuirassier, a normally rational man who has been driven by his quest for revenge beyond the borders of rationality. The point of view is by no means so sharply contrasted in the legend of Shuran; but when Zarnitsky narrates the mystery he is in a disturbed state, and this contrasts effectively with his calmly stated explanation. Both contrasts in point of view lead the reader from the temptation to compare the supernatural story with the natural explanation, and they deceive him into accepting the explanations without analyzing them.

Marlinsky completely ignored a fourth point made by Scott in his memoir. In Scott's opinion, the Gothic Revival was a resumption of the tradition of the medieval Romance, and tales of horror are best treated in medieval surroundings. Marlinsky, on the other hand, convinced that contemporary life was rich in supernatural themes, believed that no country could compete with Russia when it came to skeletons in family closets. He emphasizes this conviction several times in *The Cuirassier,* and his main narrator declares in one instance: "How unfair it is that our writers complain we do not live in a Romantic era! . . . If they would just glance into our villages and towns . . . they would find an inexhaustible source, a key purely Russian, virgin, without admixture." Marlinsky was not interested in the

those inimitable Russian devils known as *besy*. The sledgedriver's lecture on these creatures borrows heavily from general and localized terms, and these, combined with his expertly localized colloquial speech, fully justify Marlinsky's claim to an expert knowledge of colloquial Russian.

III *The Tales of the Caucasus*

Although it would not be proper to trace all of Marlinsky's literary popularity solely to the tales of the Caucasus, it was especially this fifth and last generic category that enthralled his reading public. For their wild improbability, their extreme exoticism, and their passionate tone of narration, these tales could not but have appealed to admirers of Marlinism. At the same time, precisely the extravagance and extremism of the tales of the Caucasus ensured Marlinsky's decline in the more sophisticated literary circles. Shortly after Marlinsky's death, Stepan Shevyryov noted:

Here, under the influence of Asiatic taste, which also loves exaggeration, Marlinsky's shortcomings reached their final extreme. For the passion for the variegated and the bizarre had to pass — and so it was, especially when Pushkin's muse shifted from verse to prose, and turned the Russian vernacular to that pure, transparently clear, marvelous simplicity which outdid even Karamzin. Nowadays Marlinsky no longer appeals to anyone except inexperienced youths, who are wont to be carried away by his style and curl their speech in much the same way as they curl their hair.[12]

And this is true. "Do you know," Turgenev once confessed to Tolstoy, "that I used to kiss Marlinsky's name on journal covers?"[13] Tolstoy might have confessed the same thing about his own adolescence, for it was at least partly under the influence of Marlinism that he volunteered for military duty in the Caucasus. But in one of his first literary works he remarked: "I was introduced to one of our young officers 'daredevil-Djigits' educated in the manner of Marlinsky and Lermontov. These men view the Caucasus in no other way than through the prism of heroes of our time, Mulla Nurs, and such like."[14] Marlinsky was outgrown with the adolescence of educated Russians, and it was especially Marlinism that writers like Turgenev and Tolstoy had in mind when they reacted to Romantic literature. They almost always referred to the tales of the Caucasus when professing dislike of all that was represented by Marlinsky's literary standard. The extremism, the exaggeration, the enthusiasm of these tales ensured his lasting popularity with the unsophisticated reader and his swift demise in the opinion of serious *literati.*

The tales of the Caucasus are the most extraordinarily imaginative and incredible of Marlinsky's prose tales, although at the same time they are the most authentic of all Russian literary works on the Caucasus. When Marlinsky arrived in the Caucasus in late 1829, he plunged himself into study of the area in all of its social, cultural, historical, geographical, and linguistic aspects. Perhaps no other Russian writer had a more sound knowledge of the region, and no other writer did more to educate his countrymen about their most exotic imperial acquisition. His desire to educate as well as to entertain his readers was immense, and no other Russian writer of the Caucasus — Pushkin, Lermontov, Tolstoy — can compete with his erudition.

He swiftly mastered the Persian and Tatar dialects of the region; he became an authority on Caucasian literatures and culture. Just as he had saturated his Russian and Livonian tales with authentic atmosphere, he set about now to endow his Caucasian tales and essays with technically detailed facts and lessons in the nuances of languages. In a study of Marlinsky's works on the Caucasus, the Georgian scholar Vano Shaduri has noted that "he interlaced his tales and essays with numerous historical references and ancient legends, described in minute detail the various rituals, the nature and mode of life of the Caucasus, supplied his works with a multitude of ethnographic, historical, and linguistic comments and elucidations. . . ." In Shaduri's view, "it was through ethnic facts that the writer strove to penetrate into the dynamics of life in the Caucasus."[15]

Marlinsky was upset by Russian ignorance of the Caucasus. In the preface to the Caucasian tale, *Rasskaz ofitsera, byvshego v plenu u gorcev* ("The Story of a Russian Officer in Captivity among the Mountaineers"), he complained: "We regret that there are no worthwhile testimonies about the peoples of the Caucasus. . . . But who is to blame for this if not ourselves? For thirty years we have girdled the mountains with a belt of steel bayonets; and to this day our officers have brought back from the Caucasus, instead of useful, or at least entertaining news, only swords, robes, and girdles of black silver. The most venturous of them have learned to dance the lezghinka — but beyond this, not so much as a kernel."[16]

The first important feature of the Caucasian works, consequently, is their pedagogical fervor, and it is their multitude of facts that makes them so fascinating as literary works. The amount and variety of information packed into the essays are especially impressive. In "Put' do goroda Kuby" ("The Route to the Town of Kuba," 1834) Marlinsky notes: "What I say about the Dagestanians does not apply to the Chechens or the Circassians. Every people in the Caucasus has its own mode of warfare and brigandage, its own mores, its own customs, its own peculiar ways and whimsies." Reporting the looting of Russian churches in "Pis'ma iz Dagestana" ("Letters from Dagestan," 1831) he adds in a footnote: "A strange event occurred which proves the Circassians' respect for St. Nicholas. While looting a Russian church to the bare boards they left only a rich icon of this holy man untouched." In "Proshchanie s Kaspiem" ("Farewell to the Caspian," 1834) Marlinsky augments his poetic praise of the sea with such technical observations as: "Humboldt proved the level of the Caspian Sea is below the level of other seas by about three hundred feet; consequently the opinion that there is a subterranean connection with the Indian Ocean falls by the wayside; if this were the case, it would necessarily seek the level of other seas." In "Doroga ot stantsii Almaly do posta Mugansy" ("The Road from Station Almala to the Post at Mugansa," 1834) he notes that "the half-slippers of the Lezghins and Georgians not infrequently have a point on the heels about one-quarter length longer than during the time of Charles VII among the French *(poulins)*."

The vast majority of factual observations deal with languages. In "Letters From Dagestan" Marlinsky refers to the rebel leader Kazi Mulla as Tazi Mulla and notes that *tazi* means dog. In the same essay he uses the Persian word *Sardar* for the Russian commander-in-chief. He frequently explains the meaning of Tatar words in footnotes, observing in one instance that "a *chapar* is a messenger, a driver, a wagoner; a *chapar-khan* is a relay-station inn." In reading the essays it is possible to learn that *kervan* means "caravan," *shegin-shah* means "master of masters" and a *felakka* is "a board with two holes in which are placed the legs of a criminal — his soles are twisted upwards and beaten with a stick." In one instance Marlinsky explains that "*kar-sirty* is a snow-covered range, but *kara-syrt* and *kara-dag* mean a black range, a black mountain." A typical note is: "Eastern peoples constantly use pleonasms — *gyur, bakh* ("look, see"), *ishliady, kurtardy* ("done, finished") are heard ten times a minute." In "The Road from Station Almala to the Post at Mugansa" he notes with tongue in cheek: "I think almost every reader knows that the Turkic, or, if you wish, Tatar exclamation *gaida, gai-da* means 'well,

well now, come on there!' Those who know this will recall that they have themselves used it, exclaiming, for example, *'aida, molodets!* (they there, well done!).' From this it follows that they have been speaking and writing in Tatar perfectly, without even realizing it."

The Caucasian tales also provide a rich education in customs and languages. In *Ammalat-bek* it may be learned that Asiatics wear their knives over the abdomen and can sever a man's head with a single slice; the Circassians have been famed as doctors for centuries; mountain women do not wear veils; Circassians do not bare their weapons until the last moment in the charge; Kabardinians do not destroy property in war and are shocked when others do; Tatars give a piece of their own clothing as a gift to the bearers of good news; Moslem Tatars do not eat pork, but they love boar hunts; Circassians are socially superior to Avarians; Asiatics love puns and their languages are full of them; Avarians use bronze bullets because their guns are bronze; when a Tatar wishes to speak to his Bey he bows to the ground and places his slippers on the floor before him. A typical footnote is apt to impart such information as: "All mountaineers are poor Mussulmans, but they hold to the Sunni sects; on the other hand, the majority of Dagestanians are Shagids, as are the Persians. . . . Both these sects hate each other from the bottom of the heart."

Throughout the tale there is a quick succession of literary treatments of ethnic customs, from a raid on a Cossack settlement to a discussion of the severe upbringing of children, from a contest of martial abilities to a boar hunt, from one colorfully detailed dramatization of the life of the Avarians, Kabardinians, Circassians, Tatars, and Cossacks to another. *Mulla Nur* is characterized by the same kaleidoscopic procession of ethnographic details. Among the imaginative subjects Marlinsky treats in footnotes are beards, vodka, the absence of names on graves, Circassian horses, religious sects, and the ninety-nine names of Mohammed. The tale itself contains literary dramatizations of a rendezvous between young Caucasian lovers, an Asiatic marriage, the Eastern attitude toward women, the character of the people of Dagestan, and the Oriental atmosphere of Derbent in the evening. Marlinsky effortlessly imparts such bits of authenticity as "an Asian is like a child when a gun is placed in his hands," or "only in the midst of his family does the Mussulman dare to be himself, because his wife and children are for him objects to which he is not the least obligated."

Ammalat-bek and *Mulla Nur* are also notable for Marlinsky's preoccupation with languages. In the former tale he notes: "*Ur, ura* means 'kill!' in Tatar. There is no doubt that this call entered into our own usage during the time of the reign of the Mongols, and not at the time of Peter, the notion that it is the 'hurrah' borrowed from the English." He explains that the plural of *bek* is *begliar* and that of *aga* is *agalar*, but Russians say *begi* and *agi*. He teaches his readers to count to ten and recite the days of the week in Tatar, and even mentions that an *agach* is seven versts by horse, but only four on foot. A *kekkhud* is the equivalent of the Russian *starosta* (elder) and an *empdzhek* is a suckling or milk brother (a sort of bosom buddy). *Gakim* is doctor, *aziz* is dear, *aga* is sir and *gadzhi* is a pilgrim to Mecca. *Mulla* is a holy man, *yakhunt* is an elder *mulla*, and *imam* means holy. *Dzheud* has the same connotation as the Russian term *zhid* (Yid), and Russians are always "unwashed Russians." A footnote to the title of *Mulla Nur* explains: "A *Mulla* is not only a holy man, but any literate or learned person; occasionally it is a proper name. *Nur* means 'light' and is encountered very often in combinations of Mussulman names, for example, Darya-Nur." Marlinsky adds that *Nur-magal* means "Light of the Region, and not Light of the Harem, as Thomas Moore mistakenly named the heroine of his charming poem."

The Caucasian cycle is composed of a handful of brief or incomplete works on Siberia, a long philosophical-scientific-political-literary essay entitled *Pis'mo k doktoru Ermanu* ("Letter to Doctor Erman," 1831), ten travel-ethnographic essays remarkable for their Caucasian *paysage*, the four uncompleted chapters of the novel titled *Vadimov*, and five prose tales: *Ammalat-bek* (1831), *Krasnoe polryvalo* ("The Red Cape," 1831 - 32), *On bly ubit*, ("He Was Killed," 1835 - 36), *The Story of an Officer in Captivity among the Mountaineers*, 1834), and *Mulla Nur* (1836). The prose tales mark the crowning point of Marlinsky's career as a writer. There can be no doubt that *Ammalat-bek* is the best known of the tales of the Caucasus — in fact, it is the most well-known of all his tales — and it serves as a perfect illustration of the nature of this category.

IV　Ammalat-bek

Ammalat-bek has been included in all editions of Marlinsky's works and has been a popular seller in individual editions. The tale has been translated into German, Danish, Czech, Polish, French, and English. It was the second Russian literary work published in English in the United States. Translations in French, German, and

English were published under the name of Alexandre Dumas, père, and Dumas also published the same translation as his own original work under the title *Sultanetta*.[17] When the final serialized chapter of *Ammalat-bek* had been printed in Nikolay Polevoy's *Moscow Telegraph*, Marlinsky added a postscript in which he elaborated on the tale's origin. He admitted that he had made free use of rumors and legends, but insisted that "the event described is not an invention, names and characters are preserved with exactness."

The facts he then gave are these: In 1819 Ammalat, a young and politically important Tatar bey, was captured by the Russians and sentenced to death by the proconsul of the Caucasus and the famous hero of 1812, General A. P. Ermolov. A Colonel Verkhovsky intervened on Ammalat's behalf, however, and became his sponsor, friend, and teacher. In 1823 Ammalat murdered his benefactor and later dug up his body and removed his head. Ammalat's motives for a crime that shocked the entire region were never clearly established, but it was known that he loved an Avarian girl, Seltaneta, and the popular legend was that her father, Sultan Akhmet-khan, had demanded Verkhovsky's head in return for his daughter's hand. Ammalat-bek was killed in 1828 while participating in a suicide charge as an *abrek*, a man who agrees to risk his life in this way for a certain period of time as a way of obtaining his salvation.[18] Seltaneta lived a long life and enjoyed great fame for her role in the legend of Ammalat-bek. Marlinsky knew her personally, and he also interviewed many of the other persons who figure in his tale.

Marlinsky believed — correctly — that he should have written *Ammalat-bek* as a novel. The tale is his most difficult undertaking, and its materials are so complex that it strains the limits of the prose tale as a literary form. He revised the tale several times while it was being published, and it is apparent that the legend of Ammalat-bek is uncomfortable in the form it finally took. Nevertheless, *Ammalat-bek* is a fine Romantic prose tale. Its narrative never sags, its expository, documentary, and descriptive addenda do not detract from the fast-paced plot, and its tendency to grow out of its frame even serves to enhance the kaleidoscopic effect of the variegated materials it offers to the reader.

The tale is divided into fourteen chapters. Its plot structure adheres to actual events, although it compresses the chronology of four years into two. The tale employs a great many devices — letters, diaries, digressions, verbal landscapes, descriptive interludes, monologues, and dialogues — to both advance and expand the narrative. The main narrator is the usual stylized Marlinsky, but the point of view is varied by presentation of Ammalat's diary and the letters of Verkhovsky to his fiancée.

The story centers on the psychological development of Ammalat from a primitive chieftain to a civilized man, but this center shifts to the story of Verkhovsky. There are thus two themes — one central, the other peripheral but integral — that of the civilizing of Ammalat and, in contrast, that of the idealistic and ultimately ineffectual ideas and actions of Verkhovsky. Both characters are Romantic in the extreme — the one a fiery rebel, the other a dreamy escapist — and their mutual tragedy is their inability to reconcile themselves to their alien milieux and to bridge the gap between their diametrically opposed cultural experiences. The theme of civilized society versus the natural man is Roussellian, of course, but the Soviet critic Nikolay Stepanov is correct in his observation that "despite all the conventional coloring and decoration of the Caucasus, as he depicted it, Marlinsky understood perfectly well that this is not Jean-Jacques' utopia come true."[19]

Marlinsky was also correct in his conviction that the character of Ammalat is made clear from the very beginning. When his horse balks at a jump, the willful young Tatar smashes it to the ground with his sabre handle, shocking even his savage retainers with his powerfully impatient will. In long letters to his fiancée, the introspective Verkhovsky analyzes his hot-tempered charge, elaborating on the carelessness of his upbringing and emphasizing that "his intellect is a marvelous mixture of every absurdity, of ideas most absurd and conceptions most sensible." Coupled with constant strife between impulse and good sense is Ammalat's youth and inexperience. His lack of maturity draws him under the power of Sultan Akhmet-khan and, still in the first chapter, the crafty old Avarian succeeds in inciting revolt among Ammalat's own people. Forced to flee into the mountains, and wounded in the pursuit, Ammalat is nursed back to health by Seltaneta, and he falls in love with her.

Skillfully exploiting Ammalat's feelings, Sultan Akhmet washes away the thin veneer of civilization acquired from proximity to the "despicable" Russians, and persuades Ammalat to join a raid on a Cossack settlement. Although the Avarian leader is certain that Ammalat will become the symbol to inspire the entire Caucasus against Russian rule, the young Tatar is captured in the raid. Sentenced to death by Ermolov, Ammalat is saved by Verkhovsky, who guarantees his parole and determines to civilize him. Fascinated by

Ammalat's passionate, yet sensitive character, Verkhovsky believes that if he can win his total trust and friendship, he will be able to show the way to reconciliation between Russians and Caucasians.

Verkhovsky is the total antithesis to Ammalat. He is an idealistic dreamer but a hardy soldier — the true partner of Mechin and Pravin. He has a deep sympathy for the peoples of the Caucasus and a painful realization of the antipathy between their lusty, savage cultural milieu and his European civilization. He is a sincere man, a brave and honorable soldier, and a rational thinker who sees the injustice of Russian rule over the Caucasus just as clearly as he believes in its ultimate efficacy. But his constant dreaming and idealization of the Caucasian reality, joined with his prim sentiments, his inability to accept and sympathize with the innocent guile and savage behavior of the Caucasians, make him unfit for the task he has set himself. In his long letters to his fiancée he complains of the "savage and confining" Caucasian milieu. He partly understands Ammalat, and he succeeds in awakening the Tatar's consciousness of a world beyond his own will and instinct. He even discovers the key to Ammalat's trust — his love for Seltaneta — and Verkhovsky determines to wrest the girl away from her father, give her to Ammalat as the final proof of his friendship, and use their bond of perfect trust to tear down the barrier between their mutual misunderstandings. In the final analysis, however, he is himself unable to trust Ammalat, and he disapproves of the Tatar's sometimes savage quests for revenge, to say nothing of the ease with which he employs perfidy to destroy his enemies.

The relationship between Verkhovsky and Ammalat is a skilfully contrived microcosm of the larger relationship between Russians and the peoples they are trying to pacify. Behind Verkhovsky is Ermolov, that giant of a Russian bear whose brutal pacification of the Caucasus contradicts the admiration of the man by the younger generation of the 1820's. Ermolov's policies are summed up in his own words, as reported by Verkhovsky: "One execution will save hundreds of Russians from destruction and thousands of Moslems from treason."

Ermolov's character and policy are treated with sympathy by Marlinsky, but he does not deny that the Russians are hated, as well as respected and feared, by the Caucasians. Sultan Akhmet is especially determined there will be no peace in the region until the Russians are driven out. And as Ermolov is to Verkhovsky, so Sultan Akhmet is to Ammalat. Determined to provoke or force the influential young bey to revolt, he slowly weaves a web of Asiatic intrigues around him. Ammalat's vanity, his resentment of parole, his primitive longing for freedom, his thirst for glory, his duty to his people, his distrust of Verkhovsky and his failure to understand the Russian, and, above all, his hot desire for Seltaneta — all of these forces are craftily exploited by Sultan Akhmet through messengers in the night and meetings in the mountains. Verkhovsky's hopes for peace and reconciliation are thus in contradiction to the irreconcilable interests of larger political powers.

The tragedy of the tale is not to be accounted for in the larger scope of political policies, however. Tragedy, in Marlinsky's Romantic terms, is personal and individual: it stems from the fatal failure of the two principals to understand one another. Verkhovsky admires Ammalat and idealizes their friendship. Despite his resentment of parole, Ammalat is sincerely grateful to Verkhovsky for his life. Although both men desire sincere friendship, they are unable to overcome their respective shortcomings. Verkhovsky distrusts Ammalat's "Asiatic perfidy"; he is too overwhelmed by the idea that "the barbaric despotism of Persia . . . has cultivated in the Caucasian Tatars the most base passions, introduced the most despicable vices into their honor"; but he is too confident that, once he has obtained Seltaneta for his passionate bey, "it will be to me, to me that he will be obligated for the bliss of his life. . . ."

For his part, Ammalat is just as fatally mistaken. He interprets Verkovsky's scrupulous honesty as either a superior form of guile or a weakness. Initially, he is grateful that "Verkhovsky not only is showing me the way to knowledge, but is giving me the means to make use of it." But he is also tortured by the knowledge that "I once considered myself an important person, but now I am convinced of my insignificance." He especially resents feeling that Verkhovsky "stifles me with his irreproachable honor," and he doubts that "such a man, with all his goodness, can understand my passions. . . ." Trapped between his desire for freedom and his obligation to Verkhovsky, only his agonized conscience tells him that Sultan Akhmet is treachery, Verkhovsky — friendship; Sultan Akhmet — the slavery of ignorance, Verkhovsky — the freedom of knowledge. Unfortunately, Ammalat, unused to heeding his conscience, is guided more often by his instinctive dependence on craftiness.

The end is thus inevitable. While Verkhovsky exults over his successful scheme to obtain Seltaneta for Ammalat, Sultan Akhmet has ensured that "the poison of slander burns inside Ammalat."

Verkhovsky's mysterious actions in quest of Seltaneta are mistaken by Ammalat for some insidious intrigue against himself. Torn by doubts and suspicions, on the way to the surprise rendezvous with Seltaneta he concludes he is being tricked into Siberian exile. As the two men ride alone through a wood: "A shot rang out . . . and silently, slowly the Colonel slid from his saddle. . . . Ammalat sprang from his horse, and leaning on his smoking rifle, he gazed intently for several moments into the face of the murdered man, as if wishing to prove to himself that he need not fear that immovable gaze, those dimming eyes, the congealing blood. . . ."

And three days later Ammalat crowns the terrible betrayal: "Twisting the head of the corpse, he began to chop at Verkhovsky's neck, in an oblivion. . . . At the fifth blow the head separated from the shoulders. With great aversion he threw it into a ready sack and hastened to crawl from the grave."

There is great irony in Ammalat's belief he has revenged and liberated himself. When he goes to Sultan Akhmet, he finds the old Avarian on his deathbed. Now as fearful for his soul as he had been fearless for revolt, the dying man reproaches the young bey for his crime. Worse yet, Ammalat finds that the horror of his crime has aroused universal contempt, and even in his beloved Seltaneta's eyes he reads pity and aversion. Years later — still an outcast — he is killed during a suicide charge. The Russian who kills him is Verkhovsky's younger brother.

Ammalat-bek is not the last of Marlinsky's prose tales, but it serves well as a summation of his second period and as an example of the highest level he attained as a prose writer. For the tale exposes all of Marlinsky's shortcomings as a writer, and it demonstrates his finest talents. In its manner of expression the tale is one of Marlinsky's most hyperbolic, filled with torrid passions, exclamatory tones, declamation, and rhetoric.

Despite the tale's basis in fact, the presentation of many events and plot situations strain credulity to the extreme. The tale is, therefore, a perfect example of that definition of ultra-Romanticism as a concentration on "the extreme and the unusual." Little wonder that *Ammalat-bek* became a favorite point of reference for later criticisms of Russian Romantic works.

On the other hand, the tale is Marlinsky's most psychologically credible work. The themes of awakening of the consciousness of a primitive man, confrontation between the man of nature and the man of civilization, individual freedom, and the resentment of one man in the face of another's selfless generosity are unexpectedly sophisticated themes for Russian literature of the 1830's. Nor can Marlinsky be faulted for his handling of these difficult themes. His excessive hyperbole detracts from their seriousness, but he delves deeply into his thematic materials and illuminates nuances of human behavior in a way that shows care and thought. He does not falter once in his adroit handling of the mechanisms by which an author conveys theme through plot situations: Ammalat's resentment of parole, suspicions of Verkhovsky, desire for Seltaneta, and longing for freedom are expressed well in his diary and demonstrated skillfully in his actions. Ammalat stands out clearly as a child of nature whose metaphysical consciousness has been awakened deliberately and irrevocably. And his tragedy — his failure to reconcile his newly-awakened conscience with his savage upbringing — is handled masterfully in plot development, exposition, clever shifts in point of view, and his own tortured psychology. All of the motivations for the final murder are fully exposed and explored in advance, and they are developed inexorably toward the tale's climax. The situations, in fact the entire tale, are ironic, and Marlinsky treats this irony credibly. The tale is Marlinsky's most famous, it is his most extreme, and it stands as the finest illustration of his talents as Russia's first beloved writer of prose tales.

CHAPTER 5

A Poet of the Pushkin Period

THE division of Alexander Bestuzhev-Marlinsky's life into two literary careers — the young Bestuzhev whose most important contribution was his literary criticism, and the mature Marlinsky who is remembered almost exclusively as Russia's first modern writer of prose tales — takes on a particularly distinctive character when it is applied to his poetry.

The poetry of Alexander Bestuzhev — written between 1817 and the end of 1825 — is of dismayingly poor quality, whereas the poetry of Alexander Marlinsky can be counted among the best verse works of the years 1827 to 1837. While the early poetry can be defined as Romantic only in the revolutionary songs he coauthored with Kondraty Ryleev, the later poetry of Siberian exile and Caucasian exoticism is written in an opulently luxuriant Romantic manner. The poetry of the early period is unimaginative in choice of genre, stereotyped in diction and devices, and awkward in phraseology and versification, while the poetry of the later period is sometimes totally original in genre, individualistic in theme and enunciation, and smooth and graceful in style. The difference between Bestuzhev-poet and Marlinsky-poet is the difference between an untalented amateur struggling to learn the principles of versification by rote imitation and a confident master of verse who has a personal experience to convey and proceeds to do so with depth and originality. There is so much distance between the two poets and so few points of contact between them in form and genre, style and diction, theme and statement, that they might just as well have been two different figures in the history of Russian poetry.[1]

I   The Early Efforts

Because his life was so nomadic, Marlinsky's literary heritage was left in a chaotic condition at the time of his death. Only after a century of painstaking scholarship, particularly in the Soviet period, it became possible to publish the carefully compiled, edited, and annotated Poet's Library (Biblioteka poeta) edition of his poetry.[2] He probably wrote a great many lyric poems that have not survived, and those that did survive are modest in number. The edition contains forty-four original lyric poems, and sixteen lyric verses translated, imitated, or rendered from French, German, Tatar, Azeri, Georgian, Persian, and Yakut (but not, surprisingly, from English, the foreign language he liked best). Although five poems of this basic group (three of them translations) were published anonymously, they have been convincingly ascribed to his authorship.[3] To this basic group of sixty lyric poems may be added twenty "sets" of epigraphs and verse passages in the various prose works. Although it is possible to break this latter count down to twenty-seven separate verse passages and twenty-two epigraphs, it is best to consider them as sets, especially since they cannot always be extracted from their contexts without disrupting their unity. A third group of lyric poems consisting of five "Agitational Songs" and seven "Under-the-Saucer Songs" (*podblyudnye pesni*) were coauthored with Kondraty Ryleev as part of their Decembrist activities. A final verse category is represented by the fragments of an uncompleted Romantic verse tale, *Andrei, Kniaz, pereiaslavski* ("Andrey, Prince of Pereyaslavl") written in 1827.

Marlinsky once remarked that "I am a true microcosm [of my age],"[4] and his value as a microcosm of literary activity during the Romantic period is especially evident in his choice of verse genres. In his early poetry there can be found a number of traditional Neoclassical genres — odes, satires, burlesques, epigrams, and even charades. He also wrote a number of lyric poems in the sentimental-elegiac vein of Karamzin and his followers — Romantic elegies, love lyrics, and the so-called "friendly messages" or verse epistles favored by the members of the poet-friendship society known as *Arzamas*.

The Civic-Decembrist revolutionary songs written with Ryleev are undoubtedly the best of the early efforts, and these are accompanied by patriotic verses on historical themes, including a *duma*, the lyric verse genre known as the "meditation" and cultivated as a speciality by Ryleev.[5] There are a few other commendable lyric poems of the early period, with some good lines scattered throughout the early verse. But, only after the Decembrist revolt, from 1827 to 1830, did Marlinsky begin to write fully mature Romantic poetry. While his "Romantic-historical" verse tale is not sufficiently complete to evaluate fully, except to say that it is not particularly impressive as a narrative, it contains some of his finest lines and stanzas.

Among the Romantic lyric genres he cultivated are his excellent love poems, especially a series of translations from Goethe, his plaints of exile on the theme of individual isolation, his nature poems, and his poetry of "Death and the Grave." The most unusual of Marlinsky's genres are his folk poems, including a charming Yakut ballad and, of particular interest, the fierce Caucasian war chants and songs he wrote just before his death. Closely related to these are the translations he did from the various languages of the Caucasus — efforts which have made him important in the literary history of these nationalities. And finally, there are the many epigraphs and verse sets, the latter, a variety of generic ventures ranging from Sentimentalist love elegies and epistolary declamations to patriotic rhetoric.

Perhaps the quality of the early poetry is most readily demonstrated by Marlinsky's versification methods. By the late 1810's Russian poetry was already blessed by such major poets as Derzhavin, Karamzin, Zhukovsky, Davydov, Batyushkov, and such younger poets as Pushkin, Vyazemsky, Küchelbecker, Griboedov, Baratynsky, and Yazykov had begun to raise Russian poetry to the high peaks it reached during the Romantic period. None of these poets made such an unimaginative and literal use of syllabo-accentual versification as Marlinsky. Of his first thirty-one poems, only three are in a meter other than iambic, and most are in iambic-tetrameter quatrains.

His initial understanding of the principles of versification is annoyingly pedestrian. He made rare recourse to pyrrhic feet: a sign that he understood poetry as meter, rather than rhythm. The rhythmic monotony of his early poems is thus both perceptible and obtrusive. In the poem *Mikhail of Tver* (1824), for example, 148 of the total of 180 iambic feet are stressed, and 14 of the 45 iambic-tetrameter lines are rigidly given all four stresses. The rhythm of the poem is all the more monotonous in that of the ten rhymed couplets of the first stanza, seven share identical stress patterns. This fidelity to meter would be fine in German, which is essentially a "binary" language, but it severely inhibits the natural rhythm of Russian. Clearly, like Lomonosov in the eighteenth century, the young Bestuzhev understood the rules of syllabo-accentual versification all too literally; he seems not to have noticed that Lomonosov had the artistic sense not to obey his own precept that all stresses be honored.[6] Added to these metric sins is the unavoidable fact that he had absolutely no instinct for degree of stress and no appreciation for the delicate relationship between meter and rhythm.

The diction of the early poetry is also disappointing. All of his poetry in the sentimental-elegiac vein and most of the poetry written after his experimentation with Neoclassical genres is thoroughly Karamzinian in diction and phraseology. Marlinsky's early poetry is far more profoundly influenced by Karamzin than his prose tales. The first poem in the Poet's Library edition begins with the line, " 'neath the camp a comely youth," and contains such other affectedly Sentimental lines as, "With his curly locks/The evening breeze doth play," and "O little breeze, thou shalt fly/To my beloved with these tidings."

The second poem, *I Seek Myself a Loved One*, is also noticeably pseudo-Karamzinian. Such lines as, "With arrow Cupid doth smile," and such epithets as "in fiery eyes," "pearls of tears," and "leaves of roses," as well as the last melodramatic line, "Or I shall perish," are in the tradition of Russian Sentimentalist poetry at its worst. Moreover, Marlinsky is so transparently imitative of what he naïvely believed to be current fashion that he has all the faults and none of the strengths of his teachers. In no way can he be said to have reached the best standards of such Sentimentalist poets as Karamzin and Dmitriev, or such sentimental-elegiac poets as Zhukovsky, Batyushkov, or Vasily Pushkin. He regularly used such outdated grammatical devices as the attributive use of short-form adjectives long after this practice had been abandoned by such contemporaries as Pushkin and Yazykov, and even by Derzhavin in the late eighteenth century. He was frequently hard put to reconcile his syntax with metric demands, and he often forced a stress. Many devices seem to have no other purpose than to force agreement between syntax and meter, and they are thus nothing more than crutches.

But perhaps it is not fair to treat Marlinsky too harshly for his early shortcomings as a poet. His contemporaries for the most part had ample opportunity to polish or destroy their early poetry. Marlinsky's sudden death denied him this grace, as Lermontov's denied him, and there are more than just a few indications of talent in the early poems. His sardonic wit, which stood him well as a critic, was effectively expressed in his poetry too. *To a Certain Few Poets* (1819), a satire in the Neoclassical vein, is a sustained effort directed against the slavish imitation of foreign literature and an attack on the lack of contemporary appreciation for such Russian poets as

Derzhavin, Karamzin, and Zhukovsky. Especially good for its wit is *An Epigram on Zhukovsky* (1824), an expression of Decembrist disapproval of the older poet's status at the court of Alexander I. This sardonic criticism was for many years ascribed to Pushkin, while Zhukovsky accused the journalist Faddey Bulgarin of writing it.[7] The piece is written in six iambic lines of mixed lengths with an ababba rhyme scheme (indicative of Marlinsky's decreased dependence on couplets), and it accuses Zhukovsky of being a lackey. Particularly effective is the final two-foot line which plays on the title of a poem by Zhukovsky, *The Poor Singer*. The exclamation "Poor singer!" is a *double entendre:* Zhukovsky is a pitiful person and a poor poet at once.

II The Civic-Decembrist Verse

It was apparently under the influence of Ryleev and the Civic trend of the Romantic movement that Marlinsky began to develop as a poet and break free from his erroneous assumptions about verse creativity. His growth is especially evident in the revolutionary songs and in his poetry of the mid-1820's on Civic-Decembrist themes. It is undeniable by 1827, when Marlinsky wrote *Andrey, Prince of Pereyaslavl*. The poem *Mikhail of Tver*, actually a *duma* similar to Ryleev's *duma* of the same title, is a case in point, even despite its metric shortcomings. Based on Karamzin's treatment of the execution of Mikhail Yaroslavovich, Prince of Tver, by the Tatar Khanate in 1318 *(History of the Russian State*, volume IV), it is an outright glorification of the Russian past with all the over- and under-tones of the patriotic nationalism expressed by the Romantic Civic poets. It treats a martyred Russian hero and an equally martyred Holy Russia, and such phraseology as "evil, predatory khans" and "the violent tyrants over Russia" are well suited to its tone and theme. The poem uses historical grammatical forms for stylistic effect, and these are far more effective to the theme of Slavic antiquity than to the sentimental-elegiac poems.

A much finer poem is Marlinsky's Civic treatment of the figure of Alexander Nevsky in a verse passage of the early prose work, *Listok iz dnevnika gvardeyskogo ofitsera* ("A Leaf from a Guard Officer's Diary," 1821). The poem demonstrates an increasing appreciation of euphony; and it has a more flexible rhythm, a skillful use of repetition and syntactic parallelism, a smoother syntax and blending of worlds, and a more sophisticated stanzaic articulation. Its lines are swift and vivid:

> And the knights turned tail,
> And captives, and blood, and corpses showed their trail.
> Nor is there refuge from destruction
> Amidst the boundless ice-floes,
> And Alexander, like an avenging angel,
> Pursued, struck down, destroyed his foes.

Marlinsky was very much interested in a recently discovered account of Nevsky's victory over the Teutonic Knights, and his verse passage enhances his own account of the event.

As a group of poems, the "Agitational Songs" and the "Under-the-Saucer Songs" are a chief expression of Civic Decembrism, and they are usually counted among the most famous of all Russian revolutionary songs. As a genre, they belong to a tradition that was still new in Russian literature of the time. At the turn of the century Denis Davydov wrote four quite sharp political fables and satires, including especially *The Eagless, the Pheasant, and the Partridge* (1804), for which he was given swift transfer to a remote military outpost. Pushkin's political verses, particularly "*Noel*" *Hurrah!* and *The Dagger*, are important contributions to this tradition. Katenin's *Our Fatherland Suffers*, only a fragment of which has survived, Prince Vyazemsky's *Ay-Da Tsar*, and Yazykov's *The Inspiration of Proud Freedom* are only three of the many poems of a political-revolutionary nature, which along with the songs of Marlinsky and Ryleev laid the foundation of a tradition so important to Russia. The revolutionary songs were written between 1823 and 1825, the period in which Marlinsky and Ryleev collaborated most closely in their Decembrist and literary activities, and they quickly became accompaniments to champagne and oyster banquets. The "Agitational Songs" were first published abroad by Alexander Herzen in 1859, in his own *Polar Star*. Most of the "Under-the-Saucer Songs" were lost to literature until 1950 when copies were found in the Ostafevsky Archives of the Vyazemsky family.[8] Exactly which song or part of song was authored by which poet has never been clearly established, but Soviet scholars have done a great deal of excellent textological work in the reconstruction of their precise texts from a variety of manuscripts and hand-written copies.[9]

It is difficult to decide which is the best feature of the revolutionary songs: their rollicking cadences, their lusty slang and jargon, or their political sensationalism. The songs are usually based on available folk tunes or popular tunes of the day,[10] and their cadences are achieved by an adroit counter-pointing of different syllabo-accentual lines:

> Téll me, sáy,
> How tsárs are sláin
> in Rússia.

The shortness of the lines, the emphasis on pungent rhymes, and the careful stanzaic articulation all create a jeering, raucous delivery, and the uproarious tone is heightened by the use of slang, puns, and blunt rhetorical questions. The jeering tone is strengthened by single-line, single-word rhymes, and some songs — *Our Tsar Is a German Russian*, for example — are accompanied by exuberant refrains:

> Ay-da Tsar, ay-da Tsar,
> Orthodoxy's Star!

The articulation of stanzas is frequently based on metrically identical patterns, so that each song becomes a jeering chant which repeats different motifs in identically repetitive ways.

While the "Agitational Songs" are aimed totally at a sophisticated audience, the "Under-the-Saucer Songs" appeal to soldier and peasant. In fact, the former are far too sophisticated for their presumed purpose — agitation and propaganda — and only the latter could have been intended to incite the people against the autocracy. Perhaps this can be seen most clearly in their different modes of diction and use of slang.

The "Agitational Songs" are unrestrained attacks on contemporary political leaders, especially the tsar, and while their slang is authentically "folk," the language is obviously aimed for the amusement of upper-class young men. *Akh, It Makes Me Sick*, an attack on the banality and brutality of the Russian autocracy, is sung in the voice and from the point of view of Russian serfs. It complains of the "Russian lords" who "rob us shamelessly" and "strip our skins." Russian landowners are "thieves, fleecers, they suck our blood like leeches." In every way — devices, articulation, metric mixtures, use of language — these songs are purely literary. The "Under-the-Saucer Songs," on the other hand, are simple — they are composed either of a few long lines or many short lines — and they are all in folk rhythms. Their folk origins and their colloquial appeal are indicated by their use of jargon and slang for everyday tools and labors. Their raucous tone is reinforced by heavy use of such exclamations as *akh! ay da tsar*, and *oy, oy, oy!* They deal with such subjects as maidens, merchants, soldierly gossip, and even a fable of two rainbows.

The appeal of the two groups of revolutionary songs to different social classes is demonstrated even more convincingly by their third prominent feature — their political sensationalism. While the "Under-the-Saucer Songs" make no mention whatever of current political events, the "Agitational Songs" are based on court scandals and St. Petersburg gossip. They are political lampoons with little restraint in their attacks on people. *Akh, Where Are Those Islets* is a ringing satire on St. Petersburg and the court. It contains attacks on the Grand Duke Constantine, the former tsar's minister Speransky (who headed the subsequent investigation of the Decembrist affair), the publisher-monopolists Grech and Bulgarin, and such government officials as Magnitsky, Mordvinov, and Izmaylov. *Tell Me, Say* jeers offensively at Russia's history of palace revolts and the well-known possibility that Alexander I may have been a tacit accomplice in the murder of his own father, Paul I. *Our Tsar Is a German Russian* ridicules Alexander I personally for his "tight uniform," his hostility to enlightenment, his authority "in the stables," his gendarmes and stockades, and his ministers. Count Arakcheev is dubbed "that villain of villains," Prince Volkonsky is "that little old lady." The "Agitational Songs," widely disseminated in Russian political and literary circles, were cited as a most serious crime by the commission which investigated the Decembrist conspiracy. Although neither of the two groups of songs were used for the purpose of inciting revolution among the masses, their jeering tones, their cutting accusations, and their personal insults directed at powerful persons could not be easily forgiven.

III   *The Romantic Verse Tale*

Marlinsky's single attempt to write a Romantic verse tale — the uncompleted *Andrey, Prince of Pereyaslavl* — belongs firmly to the Civic tradition, but it is also significant as an indicator of his ambition to join the ranks of Pushkin, Baratynsky, Ryleev, Küchelbecker, and others by writing a great work in this, the most important genre of the 1820's. The fragments, written in 1827 while Marlinsky was still in prison, are in keeping with his interest in history, with his historical prose tales, and with one of the most prominent literary trends of the time — the interest of all men of letters in the history of their country. Beginning in the very early eighteenth century, particularly with Feofan Prokopovich's *Tragicomedy "Vladimir"* (1705), and later with Sumarokov's Neoclassical historical dramas *Vysheslav* (1768), *The False Dmitry* (1771), and *Mstislav* (1774), cultured Russians took an interest in their own national peculiarities and in their national past. The trend was given great impetus at the turn of the century by Karamzin, first in his historical prose tales — *Natalya, the Boyar's Daughter* (1792) and *Marfa Posadnitsa* (1803) — and then in the writing of his *History of the Russian State.* Ozerov's early nineteenth-century historical dramas were a reflection of the Russian interest in history, as were a great many épopées on historical themes written in the eighteenth and early nineteenth centuries.

But the greatest difference between the Russians of the eighteenth and nineteenth centuries was, as Marlinsky himself always emphasized, the awakening of national consciousness during the War of 1812. The national trauma had a great impact on Ozerov's dramaturgy, and it shaped Katenin's ballads on historical themes. The trend was continued in the 1820's, most notably in Pushkin's drama *Boris Godunov* (1824 - 25) and his historical verse tale *Poltava* (1828). The historical works of the Decembrists, particularly Ryleev's *dumy* (1821 - 23), were important, as were the *dumy* and other historical poems of such other Decembrists and Decembrist sympathizers as Katenin, Yazykov, Pushkin, Baratynsky, Küchelbecker, as well as those of such other poets as Karamzin, Zhukovsky, Gnedich, and Pletnyov. Ryleev's *Voynarovsky* (1823 - 25) was of central importance to the Civic historical trend.

Andrey, Prince of Pereyaslavl was left in such a raw state that Marlinsky had no intention of allowing it to see print. In an explanation to the writing he once noted: "I grew tired of flitting like a dragonfly from subject to subject for lack of patience to connect them smoothly. Two months later my discarded work seemed beautiful to me, in another two, good, then fair, and in half a year I found it scarcely endurable."[11] Nevertheless, in 1828, without his permission, the first chapter of the verse tale was printed, and its hapless author, far off in Siberia, could do nothing but grit his teeth in rage.[12] It was only in 1832, through the good offices of Nikolay Polevoy, that Marlinsky was able to publish a protest in the *Moscow Telegraph:* "Picture to yourself a lunatic coming to his senses in a full theater dressed in nightcap and gown, and you will still not have a thorough idea of this author who has been brought into public in such a state of deshabille."[13]

But despite the fragmented and unpolished condition of the verse tale, it is not without charm. It is impossible to speak of a plot, of course, but the main theme is well enough developed to appreciate, and there are sensitively developed motifs. Set in Kievan Russia of the twelfth century, its central conflict is between Andrey, Prince of Pereyaslavl, and Lyubomir, a warrior who hopes to gain Andrey's suzerainty by siding with Vsevlad, Prince of Kiev, in a plot to subdue Pereyaslavl.[14] It is apparent that the conflict is between "the people" and "autocracy," for Andrey is clearly a ruler by and for the people. The lines of conflict are drawn just as clearly between generations, for both Svetovid, son of Lyubomir, and Roman, a young warrior, are attracted to the side of the young, heroic Andrey.

Civic valor is evident in both the tone and content of the verse tale. Andrey selflessly subordinates his own glory to the common good of ancient *Rus*, that good being clearly defined as the welfare of the people. When Roman comes as an emissary of Vsevlad, Andrey declaims:

> Emissary! Our soul is the price
> We will pay for the blood of the people!
> It is not glory, but vengeance
> On that beast, that I have forsaken.

Again, after Roman witnesses a colorful demonstration of popular love for Andrey, the latter declares:

> The people's praise is joy for me;
> Is it I, Roman, who ought fear evil?
> Their succor is my throne,
> Their love is my protection!

The motifs connected with Andrey are based on renunciation of both glory and revenge for the sake of respite from the internecine strife which characterized the political system of Kievan Russia. Andrey willingly denies himself revenge on Lyubomir, the murderer of his father. In direct contrast to his determination to maintain the peace are the motifs connected with Lyubomir, first his willingness to sacrifice Russia for his own ambition:

> Our band is strong, our friends dependable,
> To us will come mobs of Polovtsians,
> And Polish magnate-*pans*
> Eagerly proffer their arms.

and then his calculating pursuit of power:

> Andrey shall fall, again Lyubomir
> Will take the ruler's mantle;
> And power awaits my friends,
> And the world will be our feast.

Secondary to these barely connected motifs of the main conflict
are well-developed motifs of lesser themes. The theme of youth and
purity in the friendship between Roman and Svetovid is always
presented in a pastoral setting. The theme of glorious *Rus* is present
in recurring motifs and descriptive stanzas. Even though the imprisoned Marlinsky was unable to support his verse tale with the
careful research that is so important to his prose tales, he succeeded
in catching a great deal of historical vividness. Worthy of mention
here are a song of the hunt, in amphibrachic and anapestic lines, and
a fisherman's song in trochees. Well-developed also are motifs on the
perishability of glory, the devastation of war, and death and eternity.
Underlying and supporting these themes and motifs are some undeniably beautiful lines and a few unusual metric devices. To the
latter belong frequent initial linear inversions and several lines
remarkable for their unusual metrical and lexical construction.

There are a great many lines and stanzas which serve to illustrate
that this verse tale could have become an appreciated work of Russian Romantic literature, but perhaps one stanza in particular, a
stanza which provided several lines and images for Lermontov's
famous lyric poem *The Sail* (1832), gives some sense of the tone and
imagery characteristic of the entire verse tale:

> The lone sail whitens,
> Like the wing of a swan,
> And sad is the clear-eyed wayfarer;
> At his feet a quiver, in his hand the oar.
> While with a carefree smile,
> Sprayed with flying foam,
> Fearlessly 'midst the surging waves
> Into the storm he rushes.

There is a profusion of Romantic virility in the fragments, and at
the same time a grace and resonance to the lines. They have those
same qualities defined as "vibrant" in Lermontov's verse tales, with
none of the formal clarity of Pushkin's. The Civic flavor is also
strong, and they remind the reader that the Civic poetry of the
Romantic period was written with sincerity and with one of the first

truly sympathetic attitudes toward the Russian people. The tale's Civicism can be detected in the glorification of ancient *Rus* and the loftily elevated style of Andrey's monologues. Probably the latter feature accounts for a lack of tonal differentiation in the speech of different characters, and a failure to distinguish even between character speech and narration. Nevertheless, Marlinsky's good taste and instinct for poetry — so contradictory to his early talent — can be felt in line after line of excellent verse, and this prevents the declamatory tones from irrevocably marring the esthetic value of the work as a whole.

IV   *The Poetry of Exile*

The verses written during Marlinsky's Siberian exile, from 1827 to 1829, are on a totally new artistic level, revealing a fully mature Romantic creativity. His sojourn at Yakutsk along the Lena River was one of great verse productivity. One of the finest results is his rendering of the love poetry from Goethe's *West-Östliche Divan*. To this series belong *Youth (An Imitation of Goethe)*, *From Hafiz*, *From Goethe (From Persian)*, *From Goethe (Imitation)*, *Suleika*, *From Persian*, *Always and Everywhere*, and *Magnet* (all 1828). The lyrics usually have stanzas of four, six, or eight lines, frequently written in trochees. Each lyric is remarkable for its clarity and simplicity, but the rich mellifluousness (to use another term applied to Lermontov) makes the poetry fully Romantic, so that the elegance is nothing like the disciplined poetry of Pushkin. The poems are also remarkable for their sensuousness and their swift, brief eroticism, as indicated, perhaps, by the second stanza of *From Goethe (Imitation)*:

> But in the dark, and in the quiet,
> I find thee, unseeing,
> By the heat of thy virgin's soul,
> By the sweet sensuousness of thy kiss.

The lyrics of this series are all marked by their sensitive alliteration, their grace of syntactic parallelism, and their subtle coordination of rhythm, syntax, intonation, and semantics. They are fully sensual, with none of the cloying sentimentality that mars the early poems.

More in keeping with Marlinsky's fate and his forbiding milieu is a new contemplative, even religious tone to his poetry. For now we find in his poetry a fine post-Zhukovsky treatment of the Pre-romantic theme of death and the grave. The first hint of this new quality appears in the poem *Inscription over the Grave of the Mikhalevs in the Yakutsk Cemetery*. Indicative of theme and tone are the lines embodying the idea that "neither here nor there have you known separation, nor known the sufferings of those who loved you." Further indication of Marlinsky's attitude, as well as a religious flavoring, is to be found in the brief and sudden statement of the final line: "And we shall all be reunited in the embrace of our Creator." Marlinsky's conception of the theme of death and the grave is quite different from that of Zhukovsky, who introduced into Russian poetry the melancholy tone and pastoral descriptiveness of the German and English Romantics and Preromantics, particularly through his translation of Gray's *Elegy Written in a Country Churchyard* (1802). Marlinsky refused to be passive in the presence of the mystery of death, thus disassociating himself from Zhukovsky's less passionate poetic manner. Perhaps this is most forcibly illustrated by *The Skull* (1828), in which Markinsky demands "tribute from the grave" and calls out to it from "the secret limits of existence" which is also "my own spirit — the peer of all eternity." Clearly, Marlinsky would not be content to surrender passively to the grave, and in this regard the source of his theme is important.

The primary origin is, of course, the soliloquy from *Hamlet*, but Marlinsky's direct response is to Evgeny Baratynsky's interpretation of the theme in his own poem *The Skull* (1825). Both men were aware of Zhukovsky's poetry of death and the grave and, even more important, of Byron's rebellious expression of the theme in *Inscription on a Skull Goblet*. Marlinsky also had Goethe's *Faust* in mind, for his poem is fitted with an epigraph from that work. The Soviet critic N. I. Mordovchenko has examined all these relationships and concluded that Marlinsky had deep reservations about Zhukovsky's and Baratynsky's passive acceptance of death. In contrast to their poetry on the theme, his own poem is also the epitome of the cult of "I."[15]

From the theme of death and the grave, Marlinsky turned to the enigma of his own fate, first as a recurring motif, then as a theme which came to dominate his poetry of exile. The two themes are related — both are contemplative and both have an introspective concern with death and eternity. But where the first is religious, sometimes morbid, even demoniac, the second becomes more and more the lament of an isolated man who yearns desperately for "homeland and freedom." The plaint of exile first appears as a motif in 1829, in the poem *On a Name-Day*. Although it is a promise to be

cheerful for the sake of the addressee's name-day, it is nevertheless
plaintive in tone, as in the opening lines delivered by "a reluctant
guest in alien land." In the very next poem, *To Lida*, the motif is ex-
tended to encompass the desperation of a young man cut off from a
normal life, and the same note of desperation engulfs another poem
of 1829, *To E. I. Bulgarina:*

> Why, oh why did you desire
> To rouse my heart anew,
> And in your fleeting script
> My grief anew inscribe?

Yet despite this reproach, there is still a note of optimism, even of
good humor. For Marlinsky is quite sure he will return to St.
Petersburg soon, and he likens himself in that happy future to "a
pompous goose" who will swim serenely over the lake of self-
content.

Before the year 1829 was over, however, Marlinsky's plaint of
exile had lost its optimism and become a theme centering on
homeland and freedom — two desires he now realized he was never
to fulfill. In the poem of that year, *To a Cloud*, he likened himself to
a cloud driven through the cold sky by a merciless wind. He has
given up all hope of returning from exile, and the last two lines
reveal a now total pessimism: "And I shall perish far away/From
homeland and from freedom!" The theme of hopeless personal fate
is even stronger in another poem of that year, *Shebutuy*. Drawing
attention to himself by a simile with the vivid, sounding waterfall, he
addresses himself to Shebutuy in this fashion:

> Like you, proud, rebellious,
> From the heights of my native cliffs,
> Carried away by mindless passion,
> I plunged in an abyss of destruction!

In his study of the waterfall motif in Russian Romantic poetry,
Dmitrij Čiževskij has pointed out that not only *Shebutuy*, but also a
verse passage from the prose work *Journey to Revel* and the poem
Finland (1829) are direct descendants of Derzhavin's introduction of
the motif in his *Waterfall* (1791 - 94). In Čiževskij's opinion,
Marlinsky exhibits a more mature Romanticism in his imagery, in his
"psychologization" of a natural phenomenon, and particularly in his
lyric address to a phenomenon of nature as a vital being.[16] As the

above quatrain indicates, this is true: the waterfall becomes animated for its power, its turbulence, its roaring plunge into a rocky abyss. Moreover, by so vividly "psychologizing" a mind-stunning natural phenomenon, and then likening his own feelings to its "mindless passion," Marlinsky dramatizes his own fate, his own fall from grace. *Shebutuy* is perhaps Marlinsky's most powerful expression of regret for his impetuous involvement in the Decembrist conspiracy and revolt.

V   *The Caucasian Folk Poetry*

When Marlinsky's interest in folklore is considered, it comes as no surprise that his last and perhaps finest poetry is his Caucasian folk poetry. In his poetry, even more than in his prose, he found an outlet for his love of languages, and he devoted much time and energy to translations of poetry from the various languages of the Caucasus. Almost all of his translations and renderings were added to his tales of the Caucasus, and two of the best sets of folk songs are to be found in *Ammalat-bek* and *Mulla Nur*.

The excerpts from the latter tale are a chorus sung to welcome the rain, approximately iambic, and a folk song in trochees. Both are translated from Azeri, and they cannot be appreciated out of context. The song of the rain, for example, is central to the drought, and thus to the young hero's quest into the mountains for the snows of Shah-Degh to end it. Better, perhaps because of stronger quality, is the set of verses in *Ammalat-bek*, especially the "Death Songs," which Dmitry S. Mirsky has called "a thing unequalled of its kind in the language."[17] The first song of this set is a song of Kabardinian antiquity sung by one of the tale's characters to the accompaniment of an instrument similar to the Russian balalaika. It is written in trochaic *tetrameter:*

> 'round Kazbek fly clouds,
> Like mountain eagles . . .
> Head on towards them, up the steeps
> of Uzdeney, a fleeing band flies,
> Higher, higher, steeper, steeper
> It races, by Russians smashed!
> Its trail seethes with blood.

The "Death Songs" are more unusual in that they are written for full and half choruses, each choral part written in a different meter

or even a metric mixture. The opening and closing refrain, for example, is composed of a couplet, both lines of which are hemi-stiched,
each hemi-stich composed of an amphimachris: Fame to us — death
to foe,/Allah-ha, Allah-hoo! The "Death Songs" were to be chanted
high in the mountains on the eve of battle, and they must have been
impressive when they resounded down into the valleys from above.
They call for maidens not to grieve, but to understand that their
heroes will be called to heaven, and for their "warrior-brothers" to
remember their fallen comrades at the celebration of victory.

Marlinsky's last Caucasian folk song, in fact his last literary work,
Adler Song, was written on the eve of his death at Cape Adler in
1837. The song is comprised of four-line stanzas, the second and
fourth lines being a repeat and the third a refrain common to all
twenty stanzas. The song has no metric pattern and is written to the
tune of a Russian song. Each stanza is a curse of the Russians and a
challenge to battle:

> There sails through the sea a fleet of ships,
> Like a flock of swans, a flock of swans.
> Ay, burn, burn, burn, speak forth,
> Like a flock of swans, a flock of swans.

Particularly striking is the third line, the jeering refrain with its con-
secutive stresses.

It is not difficult to offer an evaluation of Marlinsky as a poet of
the Romantic period in Russia. Taken as a whole, his poetry is
somewhat below the high standard of his time, but at its peak it compares well with even some of the best. When only his mature poetry
is considered — and perhaps this is the only fair way to appreciate
him as a poet — he can be seen as a very good lyric poet and a surprisingly excellent master of the line. Perhaps the value of this last
talent is demonstrated best by the fact that Lermontov detected
many of the finest lines and used them in his own poetry. It is essential to understand that it was at the point in his life when Marlinsky
turned to personal lyricism — to his own fate and the expression of
his own feelings — that his poetry became richly Romantic. His personal experience was, after all, unusual, and its impact on his craft
was conducive to the lyric as a genre of expression. Never once in all
the dozen or so poems devoted to the plaint of exile and the theme of
homeland and freedom did Marlinsky strike a false note, use a banal
rhyme, or communicate an affected emotion. And when we turn at

last to the Caucasian poetry, it may be said that his verses became unique, bizarre, innovational. They introduced into Russian poetry something unusual and unexpected.

Beyond these evaluations there is something else about Marlinsky's poetry. As a poet, Marlinsky was very much a man of his time. His maturing poetic attitudes and talent, his choice of verse genres, his concept of versification, and his attempts to enlarge the potentials of Russian verse all combine to make him a microcosm of the poetry of the Pushkin period and a standard of Romantic poetry in Russia.

CHAPTER 6

Conclusion

I N the second decade of the nineteenth century there were some Russian journals which had only about two dozen subscribers and probably not many more readers. There were perhaps less than two score persons in Moscow and St. Petersburg who can be significantly remembered today for their contributions to Russian letters, and the three hundred or so guests at the founding meeting of Admiral Shishkov's *Lovers of the Russian Word* in 1811 came perilously close to exhausting the audience Russian writers could count on. In the 1820's this dismaying situation had changed considerably — the decade exhibited a tempest of talent — but it is doubtful that even Pushkin could hope for readers outside the Russian cultural elite. The fact that polemics became so fierce at this time suggests that Russian critics believed they had an audience to influence, but for the most part they spoke to one another.

In St. Petersburg the world of letters was even something of a neighborhood group: the critic Orest Somov lived in the house next to the Russian-American Company where Kondraty Ryleev resided with his family on the ground floor and Bestuzhev the dragoon rented quarters upstairs; the dramatist Alexander S. Griboedov lived a short way down the Catherine (now the Griboedov) Canal, and the publisher-monopolists Nikolay I. Grech and Faddey V. Bulgarin had their homes and headquarters a stone's throw away; Pyotr A. Pletnyov was lecturing at St. Petersburg Imperial University right across the Great Bay of the Neva, Wilhelm K. Küchelbecker and Vladimir F. Odoevsky were working hard to propagate the metaphysics of Romantic Idealism in the capital, and the fabulist Ivan A. Krylov was snug in his sinecure at the Public Library on Nevsky Prospect; Pavel A. Katenin was as active in his military duties in St. Petersburg as the three oldest Bestuzhev brothers, and the Decembrist conspirators were able to meet conveniently in each others' nearby apartments. Until his banishment to the South in 1822, Pushkin was so busily present in St. Petersburg society that he earned the nickname "Cricket." This was an astonishing decade for Russian letters, but it was in many ways a golden ghetto of literary incest.

By the 1830's, however, the condition of Russian letters had changed dramatically, particularly as regards a reading audience. Russian writers were not yet able to make a respectable living from their labors, and journals regularly went bankrupt, but the reading public had grown well beyond the confines of the elite *literati*. Artisans, merchants, servants, and soldiers made book-selling a profitable enterprise for the first time in Russia. The historical novel came into great demand, and a band of "Russian Walter Scotts" gladly obliged with works aimed at less than lofty tastes. The great critic Vissarion G. Belinsky made his appearance, and he addressed himself to a plebeian audience. Russia was even blessed with an authentic peasant-poet in the person of Alexey V. Koltsov.

At the same time, Russian literature continued to develop in quality. Gogol and Lermontov began competing for Pushkin's mantle, and Pushkin remained active in all areas of literary activity until his death in 1837. A whole new generation of great literary figures — Turgenev, Goncharov, Dostoevsky, Herzen, Pisemsky, Druzhinin, Grigorev, Tyutchev — was making ready for its appearance, and Russian literature was coming alive in an otherwise dull, repressive state. This was the decade of Russia's first respectably large reading audience, and it was also the decade when prose works — the novel and the prose tale — began to take precedence over poetry. The idol of this decade was Alexander Bestuzhev-Marlinsky, and he enjoyed something no other Russian writer had yet experienced — widespread popularity.

There are good reasons why this is so. Marlinsky was active in virtually every cultural trend of his time, exerting great influence on events which determined the subsequent direction taken by his nation's literature. He was one of the activist critics of the early 1820's, which is to say, precisely during the years when so many problems basic to the development of a national literature were debated and, in part, resolved. His combination of wit, pungently expressed opinions, and erudite knowledge of his own and other national literatures, his pure enthusiasm and widely varied interests, and his indefatigable activity ensured that he could influence his contemporaries' understanding of literary events. His early prose tales made him a pioneer of Russian prose. The way in which his reputation came to dominate this genre in the 1830's could not but lead to popularity and to the opportunity to become a significant influence upon the establishment of the Russian prose tradition. The prose tale was the chef d'oeuvre of the 1830's, and Marlinsky was its master.

As both a writer and a literary theorist Marlinsky was a keen observer of European literary traditions and current events, and he did much to negotiate a cultural merger between his nation and Europe. Above all, his unrestrained enthusiasm for Romanticism and his aggressive propagation of Romantic ideas, to say nothing of the Romantic qualities of his literary manner, made his life and career an epitome of Russian Romanticism. It is not true that Marlinsky represents all Russian Romantic creativity, or that he is a perfect representation of Russian Romanticism as it actually was. But he was, as has been stated in the preface to this study, Russia's Romantic extremist, and his name did become a synonym for Romanticism in Russia.

Perhaps just because Marlinsky was so closely tied to his time and place, his reputation experienced such a swift demise after the 1830's. His extremism of personality and literary manner resulted in a total commitment to what was important at the time, especially to Romanticism. Thus, he was fated to be eclipsed along with the importance of those events, since for later generations their impact lessened. More than that, he was so closely identified with everything Romantic, that he became a natural target for those who soon set about to turn Russian literature in other directions.

Already in 1834 Belinsky launched a campaign against Marlinism, and during the next eight years he downgraded Marlinsky in equal ratio to his championing of Gogol.[1] Marlinsky's undeniable contributions continued to be valued, but those who wished to put an end to the Romantic movement set out to discredit Marlinsky too. This was the basic motivation of Stepan P. Shevyryov when he pointed out that "the fashion for the variegated and the bizarre had to pass" and that "nowadays Marlinsky no longer appeals to anyone except inexperienced youths."[2] This was the motivation also of such critics as Pyotr A. Pletnyov, Mikhail P. Pogodin, and Apollon A. Grigoriev, and the latter summed up their general view and Marlinsky's own fate with the observation that "it is impossible to read Marlinsky in this epoch because he blazed through his own like a meteor."[3] Marlinsky's popularity with the "lower-class" reader remained untouched until well into the twentieth century; he has continued to be standard fare for adolescents; he enjoyed a revival of appreciation during the Symbolist period; his reputation as a leading Decembrist ensured that he would remain important to those with sociopolitical interests; his style and themes exerted a still unsatisfactorily explored influence on such later writers as Ivan Turgenev and Leo Tolstoy; he enjoyed a surprisingly vigorous vogue in Europe in the 1840's and 1850's; and his contributions to Russian literature have made him of utmost importance to literary scholars. But after the 1830's he was never again taken seriously by important men of Russian letters.

Marlinsky's fate is a classic case of a popular writer in his own time, and more than a few scholars have attempted to explain it. Virtually every scholar has concluded that Marlinsky faded because Romanticism faded. This is true, but it does not fully answer to the reasons for such a fate. There is a more important reason, and Marlinsky himself perhaps provided a clue to it. At the time of his death Marlinsky was at work on a novel, and he believed this work would be the crown of his career. The novel was to be titled *Vadimov*, and Marlinsky completed the drafts of four initial chapters. There is no doubt that this novel was to be basically autobiographical, and in the chapter titled "Vadimov's Journal," Marlinsky's hero makes a statement which can be construed as a pronouncement about Marlinsky himself. Much of the chapter is an expression of the hero's hopes for a future novel to be offered to Russia. A thoroughly Romantic vision of what a novel should be, it reveals Marlinsky's faith in literature as a creation of life in all its manifestations of the extreme and the unusual. "Homer, Dante, Shakespeare, Byron, Goethe," Vadimov proclaims,

"a bright constellation crowning humanity, giants in which the world has so little faith! I feel that my thoughts could be peers to yours. . . . Yes, a huge boundless poem it was that I planned to inscribe: 'Humanity' would have been its title, humanity in all its stages, in all its crises. In this poem I would have fused sky and earth, raised the epochs from the dust, striven to seek out the fate of the imponderables in this time of judgments. . . . Like Dante I would have shattered the gates of hell with a glance; like Milton I would have flown to the throne of the Omnipotent and penetrated into the forbidden gardens of paradise; like Shakespeare I would have laid bare, exposed the human heart, and shown it spread out before the eyes, bloody, palpitating. . . ."[4]

The statement is significant and cardinal to understanding Marlinsky, because it shows how extreme was his commitment to literature, how unrestrained his enthusiasms, and how positive his faith in himself as a Romantic writer. It is all the more important because it shows that he set his ideals too high — so high that they could not possibly be realized. And it is this condition — the extremism of his ideals, as of everything else about him — that ensured his demise. Grigoriev was right: Marlinsky blazed so brightly through his own epoch that he burned himself up before the next.

Notes and References

Chapter One

1. Vissarion G. Belinskii, "Literaturnye mechtaniia," *Polnoe sobranie sochinenii* (Moscow, Leningrad, 1954), I, 83.

2. V. V. Stasov, "Uchilishche pravovedeniia," *Russkaia starina* (1881), XI, 409.

3. Ivan S. Turgenev, "Literaturnye i zhiteiskie vospominaniia," *Polnoe sobranie sochinenii* (Moscow, Leningrad, 1961), XIV, 16.

4. For a factually reliable fictional biography of Bestuzhev see Sergei Golubov, *Bestuzhev-Marlinskii* (2d ed.; Moscow, 1960).

5. Bestuzhev's first duty post was near Peterhof, the summer palace of the tsars; the Marli pavilion from which he took his pseudonym still stands there.

6. The "Glances" ("Vzgliady") are today considered Bestuzhev's chief contribution to Russian criticism, but as will be shown in Chapter Two they are not necessarily his most significant critical achievement.

7. N. A. Kotliarevskii, *Dekabristy: Kniaz' A. I. Odoevskii i A. A. Bestuzhev-Marlinskii* (St. Petersburg, 1907), p. 215.

8. "Pis'ma A. Bestuzheva k Viazemskomu," ed., N. L. Stepanov, *Literaturnoe nasledstvo* (1956), XL, 217 - 18.

9. Ia. I. Kostenetskii, "Aleksandr Aleksandrovich Bestuzhev (Marlinskii)," *Russkaia starina*, (1900), No. 1, 455.

10. The Decembrist movement was born about 1814 when army officers began forming discussion groups. It developed through a series of secret societies, and in 1822 was organized into two main groups, the Southern Society based near Kiev and the Northern Society in Moscow and St. Petersburg. Its ideology and programs were vague, but the more radical Southern Society was generally committed to a republican form of government, while the program of the Northern Society called for a constitutional monarchy. The left wing of the Northern Society, urged on by Ryleev, tended to demand more radical measures, including planned revolt, regicide and *sub rosa* support of the program of the Southern Society.

11. "Delo Aleksandra Bestuzheva," *Vosstanie dekabristov: Materialy*, ed., A. A. Pokrovskii (Moscow, Leningrad, 1925), I, 412 - 13.

12. Following the arrest of the conspirators and their incarceration in Peter and Paul Fortress in St. Petersburg, they were given pen and paper and an initial set of questions. Each set of answers, collated with others, served as the basis for the next stage of the interrogation. Actual hearings, with encounters between conspirators and investigators, were held for only important or unavoidable matters. The Soviets have published the records of the investigation under the above title.

13. See for example S. A. Ovsiannikova, "A. A. Bestuzhev-Marlinskii i ego rol' v dvizhenii dekabristov," *Ocherki iz istorii dvizhenii dekabristov* (Moscow, 1954), pp. 404 - 50. This is a brilliantly researched article, but I fail to see how the evidence provided by Bestuzhev himself can substantiate the view of him as a committed Decembrist.

14. The letter is considered an important document by historians and has been published in English: *Readings in Russian Civilization*, ed., Thomas Riha, (Chicago, 1963), II, 298 - 300.

15. M. K. Azadovskii, ed., *Vospominaniia Bestuzhevykh* (Moscow, Leningrad, 1951). The papers of the Bestuzhev family were collected and edited by several scholars over the years and put into their final order by Azadovskii. The original documents are kept in the Institute of Russian Literature (Pushkin House) in Leningrad and the Leningrad State Public Library.

16. M. I. Semevskii, "Aleksandr Bestuzhev v Iakutske: Neizdannye pis 'ma ego k rodnym 1827 - 29," *Russkii vestnik* (1870), No. 5, 245 - 46.

17. Ovsiannikova, *op. cit.*, pp. 412 - 14.

18. See *Vosstanie dekabristov*, I, 433: "Meanwhile, as I became a bit more experienced, I began to cool toward the Society. The impossibility of accomplishing anything and a distrust of certain people, whom I had viewed a bit more closely, convinced me of the lunacy of the adventure."

19. Ibid., p. 431.

20. Ibid., p. 433.

21. Ibid., p. 444.

22. Ovsiannikova, *op. cit.*, pp. 412 - 13.

23. *Vosstanie dekabristov*, I, 471 - 72; Ovsiannikova, *op. cit.*, p. 417. The commission concluded that Bestuzhev participated reluctantly in the ruling *duma* and that he recruited members only when pushed by Ryleev; Ovsiannikova concludes the contrary.

24. *Vosstanie dekabristov*, I, 470 - 73. The commission summarized Bestuzhev's role in sixteen charges, including: 1) he agreed to the extermination of the Imperial Family; 2) he aided Ryleev in the recruitment of Iakubovich and Kakhovskoi as assassins; 3) he took part in the planning of the revolt, but secretly attempted to dissuade Iakubovich from assassinating Nicholas I; 4) he incited the Moscow Regiment, but was not guilty of the wounding of two loyal officers; 5) he commanded the Moscow Regiment on Senate Square; 6) he further attempted to dissuade both Iakubovich and

Kakhovskoi, but loaned his pistol to Kakhovskoi just minutes before the latter used it to assassinate Governor-General Miloradovich; 7) he surrendered of his own volition; and 8) he cooperated fully with the investigation.

25. *Vosstanie dekabristov*, I, 437. The commission's recommendation (p. 473): "Bestuzhev was completely frank in his testimonies — he was the first to reveal that certain members of the Northern Society, at the instigation of the Southerners, were disposed to the criminal intentions of members of the Southern Society in the introduction of a republican form of government and the extermination of the Imperial Family."

26. Ibid. See especially testimonies 8, 10, 11, 12, 15, and 16, as well as "Delo Ryleeva," *Vosstanie dekabristov*, I, 194. The record states that their confrontation was friendly.

27. For a biography of Ryleev see N. A. Kotliarevskii, *Ryleev* (St. Petersburg, 1908), especially pp. 186 - 91. Ryleev begged his comrades' forgiveness as he was led to the gallows, and he fell on his knees to pray devoutly before he was hanged. It has never been established whether he was the Decembrist who cursed the Russian state after he and the other four fell through the scaffold and had to be hanged a second time.

28. Kondratii F. Ryleev, *Sochineniia* (Moscow, 1934), pp. 212 - 20.

29. Georg Adolph Erman, *Travels in Siberia*, 2 vols. (Philadelphia, 1850), I, 293 - 94. The translation is one part of Erman's book *Reise um die Erde* (Berlin, 1838).

30. Ibid., pp. 295 - 96.

31. See A. A. Bestuzhev-Marlinskii, *Polnoe sobranie stikhotvorenii*, (2d ed.; Biblioteka poeta, Bol'shaia seriia; Leningrad, 1961), pp. 272 - 77. Bestuzhev became fair game for literary pirates in the late 1820's. The manuscripts of the final edition of *The Polar Star, The Little Star for the Year 1826*, were stolen from among the documents confiscated by the government after the revolt.

32. Kotliarevskii, *op. cit.*, p. 217.

33. The words were delivered by a fictional character in Turgenev's tale *Knock . . . Knock . . . Knock. . . .*

34. M. P. Alekseev, "Legenda o Marlinskom," *Etiudy o Marlinskom* (Irkutsk, 1928), p. 11.

35. See the continual complaints in Bestuzhev's letters to Pavel: M. I. Semevskii, "Biograficheskaia stat'ia o Marlinskom i pis'ma poslednego," *Otechestvennye zapiski*, CXXX (1860), 122 - 66, 299 - 348; CXXXI (1860), 43 - 100.

36. A. A. Bestuzhev-Marlinskii, *Sochineniia v dvukh tomakh* (Moscow, 1958), II, 647 (Hereafter cited by the title).

37. Dmitry S. Mirsky, *A History of Russian Literature* (New York, 1958), p. 120.

38. *Sochineniia v dvukh tomakh*, II, 644 - 46. In a letter to Pavel dated 2

March 1833 Bestuzhev gave a full account of the event. A copy of the military trial record may be found in Kostenetskii, *op. cit.*, pp. 445 - 47. For a factual account see "Po povodu ubiistva Ol'gi Nestertsovoi," *Novoe vremia*, 1888, Nos. 4749, 4752, 4756.

39. *Sochineniia v dvukh tomakh*, II, 647.

40. Kostenetskii, *op. cit.*, pp. 451 - 53.

41. Ibid., p. 456.

42. Semevskii, *Otechestvennye zapiski*, CXXXI (1860), 157. Reference is to *Amours du Chevalier de Faublas* (1787 - 90) by Louvet de Couvray.

43. *Sochineniia v dvukh tomakh*, II, 639, 655, 660 - 61, 670.

44. Azadovskii, *op. cit.*, p. 223.

45. Semevskii, *Otechestvennye zapiski*, CXXXI (1860), 71.

46. For an attempt to establish the facts of Bestuzhev's death and to review all previous accounts see Iu. Levin, "Ob obstoiatel'stvakh smerti A. A. Bestuzheva-Marlinskogo," *Russkaia literatura*, (1962), II, 219 - 22.

47. Kotliarevskii, *op. cit.*, p. 215.

48. Belinskii, "O russkoi povesti i povestiakh g. Gogolia ('Arabeski' i 'Mirgorod')," *Polnoe sobranie sochinenii*, I, 274.

Chapter Two

1. For two thorough studies of Civic-Decembrist Romanticism, including Bestuzhev's position, see V. G. Bazanov, *Ocherki dekabristskoi literatury: publitsistika, proza, kritika* (Moscow, 1953) and *Ocherki dekabristskoi literatury: poeziia* (Moscow, 1961).

2. An exhaustive study of Bestuzhev as a critic is N. I. Mordovchenko, "A. A. Bestuzhev," *Russkaia kritika pervoi chetverti XIX veka* (Moscow, Leningrad, 1959), pp. 316 - 75.

3. Nikaloy I. Gnedich, "Razbor vol'nogo perevoda biurgerovoi ballady: *Lenora*," *Syn otechestva*, XXXI (1816), 3 - 22; A. S. Griboedov, "O razbore vol'nogo perevoda biurgerovoi ballady 'Lenora,' " *Sochineniia* (Moscow, Leningrad, 1959), pp. 364 - 74.

4. For a study of Katenin see V. N. Orlov,. "Katenin," *Puti i sud'by* (Moscow, Leningrad, 1963), pp. 9 - 60.

5. Aleksandr Bestuzhev, "Esfir: Kritika," *Syn otechestva*, LI (1819), 107 - 24.

6. Vil'gel'm K. Kiukhelleker, "Vzgliad na tekushchuiu slovesnost': Chast' I," *Nevskii zritel'*, I (1820), 113.

7. A. A. Bestuzhev, "Pis'mo k izdateliu," *Syn otechestva*, LX (1820), 252.

8. A. Marlinskii, "Pis'mo k izdateliu," *Blagonamerennyi*, IX (1820), 398 - 408.

9. Nikolai I. Grech, *Opyt kratkoi istorii russkoi literatury* (St. Petersburg, 1822), pp. 3 - 5, 6.

10. The word Romantic was used in Russia in the very late eighteenth

century, but it did not become controversial until the 1810's. Petr A. Viazemskii discussed the Romantic drama in 1817 and Kiukhelleker called Katenin a Romantic in 1820.

11. For an account of the Lomonosov reforms see D. D. Blagoi, *Istoriia russkoi literatury XVIII veka* (4th ed. rev.; Moscow, 1960), pp. 149 - 54, 174 - 81.

12. For an account of the Karamzin reforms see ibid., pp. 554 - 57.

13. A good study of the Shishkov-Karamzin debate is N. I. Mordovchenko, "Polemika o 'starom' i 'novom' sloge," *op. cit.*, pp. 77 - 98.

14. Katenin, "Pis'mo k izdateliu," *Syn otechestva*, LXXVII (1822), 251 - 52.

15. A. B., "Pochemu? (Zamechaniia na knigu: Opyt kratkoi istorii russkoi literatury)," ibid., pp. 159 - 60.

16. A. Bestuzhev, "Zamechaniia na kritiku, kasatel'no 'Opyta kratkoi istorii russkoi literatury,' " ibid., pp. 262 - 63.

17. Ibid., p. 263.

18. A. A. Bestuzhev-Marlinskii, "Vzgliad na staruiu i novuiu slovesnost' v Rossii," *Sochineniia v dvukh tomakh* (Moscow, 1958), II, 521 - 22.

19. Bestuzhev-Marlinskii, "Vzgliad na russkuiu slovesnost' v techenie 1823 goda," *loci. cit.*, pp. 540 - 41.

20. Bestuzhev-Marlinskii, "Vzgliad na russkuiu slovesnost' v techenie 1824 i nachale 1825 godov," *loc. cit.*, pp. 547 - 48.

21. The importance of the word *narodnost'* cannot be stressed too strongly. Discussion of the concept has dominated Russian letters to this day.

22. J. C. L. Simonde de Sismondi, *De la littérature du midi de l'Europe*, 4 vols. (Paris, 1813), I, 1 - 3, 6 - 7.

23. Pushkin was aware of Bestuzhev's use of Sismondi's theory, and reached the opposite conclusion. See "A Reply to A. Bestuzhev's Article 'A Glance at Russian Literature in the Course of 1824 and the Beginning of 1825,' " in *The Critical Prose of Alexander Pushkin*, Edited and Translated by Carl. R. Proffer (Bloomington, Ind. and London, 1969), p. 24.

24. *Sochineniia v dvukh tomakh*, II, 530 - 31.

25. [V. I.] K[ozlov], "Poliarnaia zvezda," *Russkii invalid*, 1823, No. 5, 19.

26. A. Bestuzhev, "Otvet na kritiku 'Poliarnoi zvezdy,' " *Syn otechestva*, LXXXIII (1823), 179.

27. For a detailed history of the almanac see "Literaturno-esteticheskie pozitsii 'Poliarnoi zvezdy,' " in *Poliarnaia zvezda A. A. Bestuzheva i K. F. Ryleeva* (Leningrad, 1960), pp. 803 - 84.

28. For an account of the competition between the two almanacs see John Mersereau, Jr., *Baron Delvig's Northern Flowers, 1825 - 1831: Literary Almanac of the Pushkin Pleiad* (Carbondale and Edwardsville, Ill., 1967), pp. 319 - 33.

29. Viazemskii, "O Derzhavine," *Polnoe sobranie sochinenii*, 12 vols. (St. Petersburg, 1876), I, 15 - 21.

30. *Sochineniia v dvukh tomakh*, II, 521 - 39.

31. Ibid., pp. 540 - 46.

32. Ibid., pp. 547 - 58. Ryleev and Bestuzhev planned to finish off their almanac with *The Little Star For the Year 1826*. The manuscript was confiscated after the revolt of December 14, 1825.

33. Mordovchenko, *op. cit.*, p. 371.

34. *Sochineniia v dvukh tomakh*, II, 563 - 65.

35. Madame de Staël, *De l'Allemagne*, 3 vols. (Paris, 1813), I, 285 - 87.

36. Ibid., pp. 287 - 89.

37. Friedrich Schlegel, *Kritische Schriften* (München, n.d.), p. 324.

38. Friedrich Schlegel, *Kritische Ausgabe*, VI (München, Wien, Zürich, 1961), 371.

39. August Wilhelm Schlegel, *Vorlesungen über dramatische Kunst und Literatur*, 2 vols. *(Stuttgart, Berlin, Köln, Mainz, 1967)*, *I*, 22 - 25.

40. *Sochineniia v dvukh tomakh*, II, 565 - 72.

41. Friedrich Schlegel's *Geschichte* was translated into Russian in 1829 and 1832, just prior to the writing of the 1833 essay.

42. *Sochineniia v dvukh tomakh*, II, 564.

43. Victor Hugo, "Préface," *Cromwell, drame en cinq actes et en vers* (Paris, 1827); Viktor Giugo, "O poezii drevnikh i novykh narodov," *Moskovskii telegraf*, XLVII (1832), 297 - 331, 435 - 71. The Russian translation was followed immediately by one of Bestuzhev's works.

44. *Sochineniia v dvukh tomakh*, II, 572 - 73.

45. Ibid., pp. 574 - 76.

46. Ibid., pp. 576 - 78. Bestuzhev's characterization of the Moors is taken from Sismondi, I, 63. The essay also indicates an awareness of Sismondi's remarks on Eastern worship of women (pp. 93 - 94), the introduction of alliteration, repetition, assonance, rhyme, hyperbole, and ornamentation into Western poetry (pp. 99 - 116), and elegance of thought and expression with harmony, metaphors, and hyperbole (pp. 58 - 63).

47. Friedrich Schlegel, *Kritische Ausgabe*, VI, 187.

48. August Schlegel, I, 121, 124.

49. *Sochineniia v dvukh tomakh*, II, 577.

50. Sismondi, I, 276 - 77.

51. Pushkin's uncompleted essay "On Poetry Classical and Romantic" was heavily influenced by August Schlegel and Sismondi. He ignored Schlegel's Normans and mentioned only the Crusades and the Moorish invasions as the basis of European civilization. See Proffer, *The Critical Prose of Alexander Pushkin*, p. 24.

52. *Sochineniia v dvukh tomakh*, II, 579 - 86.

53. Ibid., pp. 585, 588 - 89.

54. Ibid., pp. 591 - 93, 599.

55. Ibid., pp. 593 - 94.

56. Ibid., pp. 595 - 97.

Chapter Three

1. Belinskii, "O russkoi povesti i povestiakh g. Gogolia ('Arabeski' i 'Mirgorod')," *Polnoe sobranie sochinenii* (Moscow, Leningrad, 1954), I, 272.

2. Belinskii, "Polnoe sobranie sochinenii A. Marlinskogo," *loc. cit.*, IV, 31.

3. The American attitude toward the novella is curious. In an introduction to the three novellas published under the title *Sermons and Soda-Water*, John O'Hara suggests that "the resistance to the novella form comes from the non-professional public, the men and women who want their money's worth when they buy a book, and whose first test of a book is its avoirdupois."

4. All citations in parentheses in the text of this book are to A. A. Bestuzhev-Marlinskii, *Sochineniia v dvukh tomakh* (Moscow, 1958).

5. V. G. Bazanov, "Puteshestvie v Revel'," *Ocherki dekabristskoi literatury: publitsistika, proza, kritika* (Moscow, 1953), pp. 293 - 94.

6. S. G. Isakov, "Neizvestnaia stat'ia A. A. Bestuzheva-Marlinskogo (s prilozheniem otryvka iz stat'i 'Livoniia,' opublikovannaia v 'Nevskom al'manakhe na 1829 god')," *Uchenye zapiski Tartuskogo universiteta*, LXXVIII (1959), 269 - 83.

7. See for example A. P. Sharupich, *Dekabrist Aleksandr Bestuzhev: Voprosy mirovozzreniia i tvorchestva* (Minsk, 1962). See also N. N. Maslin, "Aleksandr Bestuzhev-Marlinskii," in *Sochineniia v dvukh tomakh*, I, xxviii - xxix.

8. Una Pope-Hennesy, *Sir Walter Scott* (n.p., 1949), p. 10.

9. For a study of the thematic relationships between Bestuzhev and Karamzin see L. A. Bulakhovskii, *Russkii literaturnyi iazyk pervoi poloviny XIX veka* (2nd ed.; Kiev, 1957), pp. 109 - 13.

10. For a study of the sources used in *Roman and Olga* see Bazanov, "Novgorodskaia povest'," *op. cit.*, pp. 307 - 308. Bazanov points out that Bestuzhev may also have consulted the Novgorod Chronicle *(Sinodal'nyi spisok)*. For a study of *Journey to Revel*, see Bazanov, "Puteshestvie v Revel'," *op. cit.*, p. 292.

11. Turgenev, *Polnoe sobranie pisem* (Moscow, Leningrad, 1961), I, 158 - 59.

12. *The Letters of Alexander Pushkin*, Translated, With Preface, Introduction, and Notes, by J. Thomas Shaw, 3 vols. (Bloomington, Ind. and Philadelphia, 1963), I, 224.

13. For the best study of the subject see V. V. Zhirmunskii, *Bairon i Pushkin: Iz istorii romanticheskoi poemy* (Leningrad, 1924).

14. Mordovchenko, *Russkaia kritika pervoi chetverti XIX veka* (Moscow, Leningrad, 1959), p. 365.

15. Ibid., p. 369.

16. Mordovchenko, "A. A. Bestuzhev-Marlinskii," in A. A. Bestuzhev-Marlinskii, *Polnoe sobranie sochinenii* (2nd ed.; Biblioteka poeta, Bol'shaia seriia; Leningrad, 1961), p. 27.

17. J. Thomas Shaw, "Pushkin's 'The Shot,' " *Indiana Slavic Studies*, III (1963), 27.

18. Shaw, *The Letters of Alexander Pushkin*, I, 224.

19. For a good comparative study of the latter influence see Carl R. Proffer, "Washington Irving in Russia: Pushkin, Gogol, Marlinsky," *Comparative Literature*, XX (Fall 1968), 329 - 42.

20. Mirsky, *A History of Russian Literature* (N.Y., 1958), p. 120.

21. I have in my possession my own copy of a typed text in modernized orthography of a third Bivouac tale. The tale is identical in form to the two authentic tales: two initial anecdotes interspersed with sprightly banter and followed by a third anecdote-story. The tale breaks off shortly after the start of Colonel Mechin's story of unrequited love. Although the plot is not completed, it has obvious connections to Pushkin's major prose tale "The Queen of Spades": a Russified German hero named Germann, a card game and desperate gamble against fate, usage of the numbers 1-3-7 known to be important to Pushkin's tale, and a few similar terms, phrases, sayings, witticisms, and other syntactical constructions. Pushkin's use of Bestuzhev's works as a close model is not unprecedented: his prose tale *The Shot* is known to be a parody of Bestuzhev's first Bivouac tale, and "The Queen of Spades" has known relationships to the political-revolutionary songs written by Bestuzhev and Kondraty Ryleev as part of their Decembrist activities. The style of the Bivouac tale is uncannily similar to Bestuzhev's unique style, and it even contains Hussarisms à la Denis Davydov similar to those employed in the previous two tales.

Nevertheless, the authenticity of this text is dubious. First, no such tale exists in the Bestuzhev family archives of the Institute of Russian Literature of the Academy of Sciences of the USSR, and I have been unable to find an original manuscript. Second, it is a tradition of literary hoaxers to forge a work of a second-level writer with connections to a major work of a major writer. (For the obvious reason that it would not be possible to forge, say, Shakespeare, but it might be possible to forge the work of a lesser Elizabethan dramatist.) And third, although the style is, as stated, uncannily similar to Bestuzhev's, and the text contains no error which would expose it conclusively as a forgery, the text does contain several inexplicable grammatical peculiarities and stylistic departures from Bestuzhev's norm. These can perhaps be accounted for by the fact that the tale is an unpolished fragment and might have been re-copied so many times that errors inevitably crept into the text. It can even be conjectured that the tale was written by one of Bestuzhev's successors or imitators. But the deviations in style and the curious grammatical usages do exist in the text, and they give rise to strong suspicions of a forgery.

I have consulted with several scholars in the United States and the Soviet

Union about this strange find, and I am in receipt of their analyses and theories. Irrespective of whether the work is authentic or fraudulent, I intend to publish the text as a curiousity, at an appropriate time and with appropriate commentary.

Chapter Four

1. Kiukhel'beker, "Dnevnik (glava VI, 1834 g.)," *Russkaia starina*, VIII (1883), 253.

2. N. A. Kotliarevskii, *Dekabristy: Kniaz' A. I. Odoevskii i A. A. Bestuzhev-Marlinskii* (St. Petersburg, 1907), p. 254.

3. "Pis'ma Aleksandra Aleksandrovicha Bestuzheva k N. A. i K. A. Polevym," ed. K. Polevoi, *Russkii vestnik*, XXXII (1861), 443.

4. Belinskii, "Literaturnye mechtaniia," *Polnoe sobranie sochinenii* (Moscow, Leningrad, 1954), I, 85.

5. Bazanov, "Svetskie povesti," *Ocherki dekabristskoi literatury: publitsistika, proza, kritika* (Moscow, 1953), pp. 389 - 405.

6. "Anna Radkliff (Iz sochineniia Val'tera Skotta)," *Syn otechestva*, CV (1826), 131 - 60, 368 - 82; CVI, 81 - 93, 260 - 72.

7. Sir Walter Scott, "Mrs. Ann Radcliffe," *Lives of Eminent Novelists and Dramatists* (London, n. d.), pp. 568 - 69.

8. Ibid., pp. 562, 563, 566, 567.

9. Bazanov, "Povest' o zamke na Kame," *op. cit.*, pp. 421 - 23. Bazanov has also pointed out connections between *The Cuirassier* and Karamzin's tale *Bornholm Island*.

10. M. Vasil'ev, "Dekabrist A. A. Bestuzhev kak pisatel'-etnograf," *Nauchno-pedagogicheskii sbornik Vostochnogo pedagogicheskogo instituta v Kazani*, I (1926), 72.

11. "Pis'ma Bestuzheva k Polevym," *Russkii vestnik*, XXXII (1861), 318.

12. Stepan Shevyrev, "Vzgliad na sovremennuiu russkuiu literaturu, stat'ia vtoraia: Storona svetlaia (sostoianie russkogo iazyka i sloga)," *Moskvitianin*, II (1842), 167.

13. Turgenev, *Polnoe sobranie sochinenii* (Moscow, Leningrad, 1961), III, 62.

14. Leo N. Tolstoi, "Nabeg," *Polnoe sobranie sochinenii* (Moscow, Leningrad, 1928), III, 22.

15. Vano Shaduri, *Dekabristskaia literatura i gruzinskaia obshchestvennost'* (Tbilisi, 1958), p. 315.

16. *The Story of an Officer in Captivity among the Mountaineers* is not available in the 1958 edition and must be consulted in one of the earlier editions.

17. Data relating to translation and publication of Marlinsky's works abroad is available in catalogues of the Library of Congress and the Slavonic Collection of the New York Public Library. It has not yet been sufficiently appreciated that Marlinsky enjoyed a wide vogue in Europe, England, and

the United States during the 1840's, 1850's, and 1860's. This topic of comparative literature deserves scholarly attention. Marlinsky's propagandizer abroad was Alexandre Dumas, père, who was notorious as a plagiarizer. Dumas visited the Caucasus in the 1850's, and there paid homage to Seltaneta's grave. There are French, German, and English translations of several of Marlinsky's prose tales under Dumas' name. Although Dumas claimed that his version of *Sultanetta* was his own work, a textual comparison shows that it is a direct translation.

18. See A. A. Bestuzhev-Marlinskii, *Sochineniia v dvukh tomakh* (Moscow, 1958), I, 622 - 23. For an exhaustive study of the writing of *Ammalat-bek* see M. P. Alekseev, "Istochniki povesti 'Ammalat-bek,' " *Etiudy o Marlinskom* (Irkutsk, 1928).

19. Nikolay L. Stepanov, "Aleksandr Marlinskii," in *Izbrannye povesti Aleksandra Marlinskogo* (Leningrad, 1937), p. 26.

Chapter Five

1. This chapter is based in part on a previously published article: "Bestuzhev-Marlinsky as a Lyric Poet," *The Slavonic and East European Review*, XLVII (July 1969), 308 - 22.

2. A. A. Bestuzhev-Marlinskii, *Polnoe sobranie stikhotvorenii* (2nd ed.; Biblioteka poeta, Bol'shaia seriia; Leningrad, 1961). All citations of poetry are from this text, hereafter cited by title.

3. Ibid., pp. 298 - 300.

4. "Pis'ma Aleksandra Aleksandrovicha Bestuzheva k N. A. i K. A. Polevym," ed., K. Polevoi, *Russkii vestnik*, XXXII (1861), 304.

5. The Russian *duma*, meaning "thought" or "council," was vaguely equivalent to the French *méditation*. The genre was based on an Ukrainian folk genre, the so-called "folk song" which began to replace the *bylina* (or "folk epic") in the late seventeenth century. Ryleev used Polish Romantic equivalents of the *duma* for his models, as well as Alphonse de Lamartine's politically oriented "Méditations." Ryleev's *duma* dramatized the fate of a hero from the Russian past who was considered to be representative of the spirit of his time and the glory of the Russian "democratic" past.

6. See Boris O. Unbegaun, *Russian Versification* (Oxford, 1956), p. 19.

7. *Polnoe sobranie stikhotvorenii*, pp. 271 - 72.

8. M. A. Briskman, "Agitatsionnye pesni dekabristov," *Dekabristy i ikh vremia*, eds., M. P. Alekseev and B. S. Meilakh (Leningrad, 1951), pp. 20 - 21.

9. See for example Iu. Oksman, "Agitatsionnye pesni dekabristov," *Literaturnoe nasledstvo*, LIX (1954); see also *Polnoe sobranie stikhotvorenii*, pp. 288 - 98.

10. See N. I. Mordovchenko, "A. A. Bestuzhev-Marlinskii," in *Polnoe sobranie stikhotvorenii*, pp. 19 - 20.

11. *Polnoe sobranie stikhotvorenii*, pp. 78 - 79.

12. Ibid., pp. 272 - 79.

13. Ibid., p. 80.

14. Andrey was the youngest son of Vladimir Monomakh, ruler of Kiev. When the latter died in 1125 he was succeeded by his son Mstislav, and then by another, Yaropolk. When Yaropolk died in 1139 a great many contenders for the throne appeared, and a great deal of blood was shed in internecine strife. Kiev was finally seized by Vsevlad (or Vsevolod), who ruled for ten years, although many of the princes refused to recognize his right to the throne. The Kievan system of succession, according to which each ruler left a city-principality to one of his sons and nephews, ensured constant strife to reunite the various cities into a unified political system.

15. *Polnoe sobranie stikhotvorenii*, pp. 30 - 32.

16. Dmitrij Ciževskij, *On Romanticism in Slavic Literatures* ('S Gravenhage, 1957), pp. 16, 22.

17. Mirsky, *A History of Russian Literature* (New York, 1958), p. 120.

Chapter Six

1. Belinskii's campaign lasted from 1834 to 1842, and he was still commenting on Marlinskii in the very late 1840's. His campaign was carried on in the articles "Literaturnye mechtaniia" (1834), "O russkoi povesti i povestiakh g. Gogolia ('Arabeski' i 'Mirgorod')" (1835), "Polnoe sobranie sochinenii A. Marlinskogo" (1840), "Sochineniia v stikhakh i proze Denisa Davydova" (1840), and "Stat'i o narodnoi poezii" (1842). See the articles in the first five volumes of V. G. Belinskii, *Polnoe sobranie sochinenii* (Moscow, Leningrad, 1954).

2. Shevyrev, "Vzgliad na sovremennuiu russkuiu literaturu, stat'ia vtoraia: storona svetlaia (sostoianie russkogo iazyka i sloga)," *Moskvitianin*, II (1842), 167.

3. Apollon A. Grigor'ev, "Vzgliad na russkuiu literaturu so smerti Pushkina: Romantizm (1834 - 40), stat'ia vtoraia," *Russkoe slovo*, III (1861), 20.

4. The text of *Vadimov* is not included in the 1958 edition and must be consulted in one of the earlier collections.

Selected Bibliography

PRIMARY SOURCES

Russkie povesti i rasskazy Aleksandra Marlinskogo. Vols. 1 - 8, St. Petersburg and Moscow: III otdelenie, 1832 - 34; vols. 1 - 8, 2nd ed., St. Petersburg and Moscow: III otdelenie, 1835 - 39; vol. 9, 3rd ed., St. Petersburg: Glazunov, 1838 - 39; *Polnoe sobranie sochinenii.* Vols. 9 - 12, 2nd ed., St. Petersburg: III otdelenie, 1838 - 39; *Vtoroe polnoe sobranie sochinenii.* 12 vols., 4th ed., St. Petersburg: Ministerstvo gosudarstvennogo imushchestva, 1847.

Sochineniia. Moscow: Goskhudlitizdat, 1935.

Izbrannye povesti. Leningrad: Goskhudlitizdat, 1937. Introduction by N. L. Stepanov.

Sobranie stikhotvorenii. Leningrad: Sovetskii pisatel' (Biblioteka poeta, Bol'shaia seriia), 1948.

Sochinenia v dvukh tomakh. Moscow: Goskhudlitizdat, 1958. Introduction by N. N. Maslin. The edition is disappointingly incomplete, and the text is based on uncorrected previous editions rather than the original manuscripts.

Poliarnaia zvezda A. A. Bestuzheva i K. F. Ryleeva. Leningrad: AN SSSR, 1960.

Polnoe sobranie stikhotvorenii. Leningrad: Sovetskii pisatel' (Biblioteka poeta, Bol'shaia seriia), 1961.

DUMAS, ALEXANDRE, père. *The Snow on Shah-Dagh and Ammalat Bey: Posthumous Romances* by Alexandre Dumas, père. Trans., Home Gordon. London: Simpkin, Marshall and Co., 1889. Translations of French versions of *Mulla Nur* and *Ammalat-bek.*

MARLINSKY, A., *The Tatar Chief; or, A Russian Colonel's Head for a Dowry.* Trans., G. C. Hebbe. New York, 1846.

"Evening at a Bivouac." Trans., Lauren G. Leighton. *Russian Literature Triquarterly,* III (May 1972), 82 - 88.

SECONDARY SOURCES

ALEKSEEV, M. P. *Etiudy o Marlinskom.* Irkutsk: Universitet Irkutska, 1928. Three essays by a leading specialist.

———. "Turgenev i Marlinskii," *Tvorcheskii put' Turgeneva: Sbornik.*
Petrograd, 1923. pp. 167 - 201. Thorough study of Marlinsky's influence on Turgenev.

BAZANOV, V. G. *Ocherki dekabristskoi literatury: poeziia.* Moscow:
Goskhudlitizdat, 1961.

———. *Ocherki dekabristkoi literatury: publitsistika, proza, kritika.*
Moscow: Goskhudlitizdat, 1953. Fully half the book is devoted to
Bestuzhev-Marlinsky; especially valuable for its tracing of sources.

BELINSKII, |V. G. "Literaturnye mechtaniia". *Polnoe sobranie sochinennii.*
Vol. I, Moscow and Leningrad: AN SSR, 1954. This 1834 article marks
the beginning of a systematic campaign against Marlinism. Despite his
merits, Belinsky contends that Marlinsky is only a popular writer, not
a good one.

———. "O russkoi povesti i povestiakh. g. Gogolia ('Arabeski' i
'Mirgorod')." *Polnoe sobranie sochinenii.* Vol. I. Belinsky attacked
Marlinsky as part of his campaign on behalf of Gogol as the star of his
"real" school. (1835)

———. "Polnoe sobranie sochinenii A. Marlinskogo." *Polnoe sobranie
sochinenii.* Vol. I Belinsky used the occasion of Marlinsky's new works
to reaffirm that the author's popularity is undeserved. He sees
Marlinsky, however, as the greatest Russian literary critic. (1840)

———. "Sochineniia v stikhakh i proze Denisa Davydova." *Polnoe
sobranie sochinenii.* Vol. IV. Belinsky relents and modifies his previously harsh criticism. (1840)

———. "Stat'i o narodnoi poezii." *Polnoe sobranie sochinenii.* Vol. V.
Belinsky denies Marlinsky's claim to either Romanticism or *narodnost'*.
(1842)

BOGDANOVA, A. A. "A. A. Bestuzhev kak perevodchik, retsenzent i kritik."
Uchenye zapiski Novosibirskogo pedagogicheskogo instituta, 1945,
No. 1, 41 - 68. Reputed to be one of the best existing studies of
Bestuzhev-Marlinsky as a critic.

BULAKHOVSKII, L. A. *Russkii literaturnyi iazyk pervoi poloviny XIX
veka.* 2nd ed., Kiev: "Radianska shkola," 1957. An invaluable source
for thematic and stylistic relationships.

EIKHENBAUM, B. M. "Proza Pushkina." *Skvoz' literaturu.* 'S-Gravenhage:
Mouton and Co. (Photomechanic reprint), 1962. Contains a comparison
of Pushkin and Marlinsky.

GOLUBOV, SERGEI. *Bestuzhev-Marlinskii.* 2nd ed., Moscow: Molodaia
gvardiia, 1960. A fictional but factually reliable biography.

LEVIN, JU. "Ob obstoiatel'stvakh smerti A. A. Bestuzhev-Marlinskogo."
Russkaia literatura, 1962, No. 2, 219 - 22. A review of all evidence
and previous accounts of Marlinsky's death.

LEZHNEV, A. Z. *Proza Pushkina.* Moscow: Goskhudlitizdat, 1937. Contains
one of the best studies of Marlinsky's style.

MORDOVCHENKO, N. I. *Russkaia kritika pervoi chetverti XIX veka.* Moscow and Leningrad: AN SSSR, 1959. Contains a chapter and other sections on Bestuzhev-Marlinsky as a critic. The chapter was used as the introductory article to the 1961 edition of the poetry.

OVSIANNIKOVA, S. A. "A. A. Bestuzhev-Marlinskii i ego rol' v dvizhenii dekabristov." *Ocherki iz istorii dvizheniia dekabristov.* Moscow: Gospolitizdat, 1954. A brilliant piece of research, but all evidence discrediting the opinion that Bestuzhev-Marlinsky was a convinced revolutionary is ignored.

PYPIN, A. N. "Sverstnik Pushkina: A. Bestuzhev-Marlinskii." *Istoriia Russkoi literatury.* Vol. IV, 3rd ed. St. Petersburg: M. M. Stasiulevich, 1907, pp. 419 - 79.

SHAW, J. THOMAS. "Puškin's 'The Shot.' " *Indiana Slavic Studies,* III (1963), 113 - 29. Compares Pushkin's short story with Bestuzhev-Marlinsky's *Evening at a Bivouac.*

STEPANOV, N. L. "Bestuzhev-Marlinskii," in *Istoriia russkoi literatury.* Vol. VI, Moscow and Leningrad: AN SSSR, 1953, pp. 563 - 77. Essentially the same as the introductory article to the 1937 edition. One of the best modern studies.

―――. *Proza Pushkina.* Moscow: AN SSSR, 1962. Contains a good comparison of Marlinsky and Pushkin.

VASIL'EV, M. "Dekabrist A.A. Bestuzhev-Marlinskii kak pisatel'-etnograf." *Nauchno-pedagogicheskii sbornik Vostochnogo pedagogicheskogo instituta v Kazani,* 1926, No. 1, 56 - 76. One of the best studies of Bestuzhev-Marlinsky as a folklorist.

ZAMOTIN, I. I. "Literaturnye techeniia i literaturnaia kritika 30-x godov XIX veka." *In Istoriia russkoi literatury.* Ed., D. N. Ovsianiko-Kulikovskii. Vol. I, Moscow, 1910, 277 - 330. A brief version of the following item.

―――. *Romantizm dvadtsatykh godov XIX veka.* 3rd ed. rev., St. Petersburg and Moscow, 1919. This chief scholar of Russian Romanticism treats Bestuzhev-Marlinsky as the representative of what he calls Romantic Individualism. Contains one of the most thorough analyses of Marlinism.

LEIGHTON, LAUREN G. "Marlinskij's 'Ispytanie': A Romantic Rejoinder to *Evgenij Onegin.*" *The Slavic And East European Journal,* Vol. XIII (No. 2, Summer 1969), 200 - 216.

―――. "Bestuzhev-Marlinsky as a Romantic Poet." *The Slavonic and East European Review,* Vol. XLVII (No. 109, January 1969), 318 - 22.

―――. "Marlinsky." *Russian Literature Triquarterly,* III (May 1972), 249 - 68.

Titles of Works
(Russian and English)

I. Historical Tales
   A. *Livonian Cycle*
   Eshche listok iz dnevnika gvardeiskogo ofitsera
   ("Another Leaf from a Guard Officer's Diary," 1821)
   Zamok Eizen
   ("Castle Eisen," 1825)
   Zamok Neigauzen: Rytsarskaia povest'
   ("Castle Neihausen: A Tale of Chivalry," 1824)
   Zamok Venden (Otryvok iz dnevnika gvardeiskogo ofitsera)
   ("Castle Wenden (A Fragment from a Guard Officer's Diary),"
   1821)
   Poezdka v Revel'
   ("Journey to Revel," 1820 - 21)
   Revel'skii turnir
   ("Tournament at Revel," 1825)
   B. *Russian Cycle*
   Listok iz dnevnika gvardeiskogo ofitsera
   ("A Leaf from a Guard Officer's Diary," 1821)
   Gedeon
   ("Gedeon," 1821)
   Naezdy: Povest' 1613 goda
   ("The Raiders: A Tale of the Year 1613," 1831)
   Roman i Ol'ga: Starinnaia povest'
   ("Roman and Olga: A Tale of Olden Times," 1823)
   Izmennik
   ("The Traitor," 1825)
II. Tales of Men and Passions
   Early Period
   Vecher na bivuake
   ("Evening at a Bivouac," 1823)
   *Noch' na korable (iz zapisok gvardeiskogo ofitsera na
   vozvratnom puti v Rossiiu posle kampanii 1814 goda)*
   ("Night on a Ship (From the Notes of a Guard Officer on the
   Return Trip to Russia after the Campaign of 1814)," 1822)

        Roman v semi pis'makh
        ("A Romance in Seven Letters," 1824)
        Vtoroi vecher na bivuake
        ("A Second Evening at a Bivouac," 1823)
        Later Period
        Chasy i zerkalo (Listok iz dnevnika)
        ("The Clock and the Mirror (A Leaf from a Diary)," 1832)
        Ispytanie
        ("The Test," 1830)
III. Sea Stories
        Fregat "Nadezhda"
        ("The Frigate 'Hope,' " 1832)
        Leitenant Belozor
        ("Lieutenant Belozor," 1831)
        Morekhod Nikitin
        ("Merchant Sailor Nikitin," 1834)
IV. Tales of Horror
        Latnik: Rasskaz partizanskogo ofitsera
        "The Cuirassier: A Partisan Officer's Story," 1831)
        Vecher na kavkazskikh vodakh v 1824 godu
        ("An Evening at a Caucasian Spa in 1824," 1830)
        Sledstvie vechera na kavkazskikh vodakh v 1824 godu
        ("Sequel to an Evening at a Caucasian Spa in 1824," 1830)
        Strashnoe gadan'e: Rasskaz
        ("The Terrible Divination: A Story," 1830)
 V. Caucasian Cycle
    A. *Tales of the Caucasus*
        Ammalat-bek: Kavkazskaia byl'
        ("Ammalat-bek: A Caucasian Legend," 1831)
        On byl ubit
        ("He was Killed," 1835 - 36)
        Mulla Nur
        ("Mulla Nur," 1836)
        Krasnoe pokryvalo
        ("The Red Cape," 1831 - 32)
        Rasskaz ofitsera, byvshego v plenu u gortsev
        ("The Story of an Officer in Captivity among the Mountaineers," 1834)
    B. *Caucasian Essays*
        "*Kavkazskaia stena*"
        ("The Caucasian Wall," 1831)
        "Proshchanie s Kaspiem"
        ("Farewell to the Caspian," 1834)
        "Podvig Ovechkina i Shcherbiny za Kavkazom"
        ("The Feat of Officers Ovechkin and Shcherbina in the Caucasus," 1824; rev. 1834)

"Posledniaia stantsiia k Staroi Shamakhe"
("The Last Station to Old Shamakha," 1834)
"Pis'ma iz Dagestana"
("Letters From Dagestan," 1831)
"Pis'mo k doktoru Ermanu"
("Letter to Doctor Erman," 1831)
"Gornaia doroga iz Dagestana v Shirvan cherez Kunakenty"
("The Mountain Road From Dagestan to Shirvan Via
   Kunakenty," 1834)
"Doroga ot stantsii Almaly do posta Mugansy"
("The Road from Station Almala to the Post at Mugansa," 1834)
"Put' do goroda Kuby"
("The Route to the Town of Kuba," 1834)
"Pereezd ot s. Topchi v Kutkashi"
("The Transfer From St. Topcha to Kutkashi," 1834)
"Shakh Gusein"
("Shah Hussein," 1831)

VI. *Vadimov,* an Uncompleted Novel (1834 - 38)
"Osada" ("The Siege")
"Vystrel" ("The Shot")
"Zhurnal Vadimova" ("Vadimov's Journal")
"Vstrecha" ("The Rendezvous")

VII. *Andrei, kniaz' pereiaslavskii*
("Andrey, Prince of Pereiaslavl," an Uncompleted Verse
   Tale, 1827)

VIII. *Some Important Critical Works*
"Vzgliad na staruiu i novuiu slovesnost' v Rossii"
("A Glance at Ancient and Modern Literature in Russia," 1823)
"Vzgliad na russkuiu slovesnost' v techenie 1823 goda"
("A glance at Russian Literature in the Course of 1823," 1824)
"Vzgliad na russkuiu slovesnost' v techenie 1824 i nachale 1825
   godov"
("A Glance at Russian Literature in the Course of 1824 and the
   Beginning of 1825," 1825)
"O romane N. Polevogo *Kliatva pri grobe Gospodnem*"
("On N. Polevoy's Novel *The Oath on the Tomb of the Lord,*" 1833)
"O romantizme"
("On Romanticism," 1827)

IX. *Minor Works (Not Treated in This Study)*
"Ob"iavlenie ot obshchestva dlia prisposobleniia tochnykh nauk
   k slovesnosti"
("Announcement from the Society for the Application of the
   Exact Sciences to Literature," 1823)
"Otryvki iz rasskazov o Sibiri"
("Fragments of Stories about Siberia," 1830 - 32)

"Istoriia znakov prepinaniia"
("A History of the Exclamation Mark," 1821)
"Rekomendatel'noe pis'mo"
("A Letter of Recommendation," 1824)
"Voennyi antikvarii"
("The Military Antiquarian," 1829
Novyi russkii iazyk
("A New Russian Language," 1833)
"O dereviannom stroenii v Rossii"
("On Wood Construction in Russia," 1825)
"Sibirskie nravy: Isykh"
("Siberian Mores: Isykh," 1831)
"Podvolzhskie razboiniki"
("The Volga Robbers," Fragment, 1820)
"Budochnik-orator"
("The Watchman-Orator," 1832)
X. Selected Poems
Adlerskaia pesnia ("Adler Song")
Akh, gde te ostrova ("Akh, where are those islets")
Akh, toshno mne ("Akh, it makes me sick")
Cherep ("The Skull")
E. I. Bulgarinoi ("To E. I. Bulgarina")
Ei ("To Her")
Epigramma na Zhukovskogo ("An Epigram on Zhukovsky")
Finliandiia ("Finland")
Iz Gete. Podrazhanie ("From Goethe. Imitation")
K nekotorym poetam ("To a Certain Few Poets")
K oblaku ("To a Cloud")
Lide ("To Lida")
Mikhail Tverskoi ("Mikhail of Tver")
Nadgrobie ("Inscription on a Grave")
Sebe liubeznogo ishchu ("I seek myself a loved one")
Shebutui ("Shebutuy")
Slava nam, smert' vragu ("Glory to us, death to our foes")
Tsar nash, nemets russkii ("Our Tsar is a German Russian")
Ty skazhi, govori ("Tell me, say")
V den' imenin ("On a Name Day")

Index

(The works of Bestuzhev-Marlinsky are listed under his name)